The Students' Literal Translations

DIE JOURNALISTEN

BY

GUSTAV FREYTAG

Literally Translated
by
Vivian Elsie Lyon

TRANSLATION PUBLISHING COMPANY, INC.

31 West 15th Street   New York City

THE JOURNALISTS

INTRODUCTION

GUSTAV FREYTAG, the leading German dramatist of his time, was born in Kreuzburg, Prussia, July 13, 1816, a descendant of a long line of Silesian ancestry. His father was Gottlob Ferdinand Freytag, a successful physician and prominent as the first Burgomaster of his city. As is frequently the case, Freytag received his poetic temperament, talent and inspiration from his mother, a clergyman's daughter of literary tastes and sterling character.

His childhood was spent among the simplest surroundings, and, like most border people, he was trained in profound loyalty to duty and country. He commenced his education under the tutelage of his uncle Neugebaur, and later attended the Oels "Gymnasium," the University of Breslau and the University of Berlin, from the last of which he received his Ph.D. degree in 1838. He passed through the usual

1

run of student experiences, including membership in the fraternity "Borussen," the fighting of his student duel and three days' confinement in the student prison.

In 1839 he was made Privatdocent at the University of Breslau, but later resigned, using as an excuse the refusal of the faculty to give him permission to lecture on German "Kulturgeschichte." With the exception of a term served in the North German Parliament, to which seat he was elected by the Liberal party of Erfurt, his mature life was devoted to literary and editorial work and he came to be recognized as the acknowledged peer of any other German dramatic critic, and the superior of any other in knowledge of the technique of the drama. His work, "Die Technik des Dramas," is still regarded as a standard, and authoritative on the points discussed. His declining years were passed in retirement at Wiesbaden, where he died April 30, 1895.

Alberti describes Freytag as "not one of the intellectual or poet princes that lift the world out of its orbit and lead it into new paths, that with one book make the whole world to shine in a new and unknown light, but he is a whole man, a real poet, in whose soul the spirit of the times is mirrored as clearly as the sun, the clouds and the stars of the night, in the deep, transparent waters of a quiet Alpine lake.''

Freytag's interest in the stage dates from the time he was ten years of age, at which time he was much impressed by the performances of a troupe of wandering players. This same year he wrote his first story, a tale relating the adventures of a shipwrecked father and children, containing traces of "Robinson Crusoe."

His partiality for the stage grew with the years, and in 1841 he dramatized the account of the wooing of Mary of Burgundy by the Archduke Maximilian of Austria, as he says, "with great ardor and joy and lack of knowledge of dramatic art." Although it brought him a first prize in a competitive contest, "Die Brautfahrt" was never a great success. In his "Erinnerungen" he tells of his own ecstasies at its presentation at Breslau and of his surprise that the audience did not seem to share his enthusiasm. Other plays, written after he had studied the stage more carefully, were "Die Valentine" and "Graf Waldemar," both of which met with approval and became repertoire plays.

His dramatic masterpiece, called "one of the few bright spots in the history of German comedy," is "Die Journalisten" ("The Journalists"), a play which, sixty

years after its initial performance, retains
its remarkable hold on the public affection. It has probably been acted a greater
number of times than any other German
play. In it are found many of Freytag's
personal observations and experiences in
journalism and provincial politics, a fact
which accounts in part for his skilful and
graphic depictment of the various situa-
tions.

The making up of a newspaper, as the
scene in the *Union* office portrays it, is a
direct contrast to that of an American
newspaper, but is true, even to-day, in a
lesser degree, of the provincial German
press. The editors, however, are scrupu-
lous, high-minded men and were used by
Freytag to combat the then prevalent ideas
regarding journalists. Oldendorf, with his
exaggerated sense of duty, his acceptance
of the nomination "for the good of the
party," is the subject of Adelheid's witty
depreciation of men and is the object of
the Colonel's vexation, though at length
the latter finds himself in the same position. The Colonel himself is a gruff, self-
willed gentleman of the military class, but
lovable in spite of all. His daughter, Ida,
is most filial, but leaves a question in the
reader's mind as to whether she is capable
of repaying a man who sacrifices his career

for her sake. Bolz, with his never-failing humor and philosophy in the midst of misfortune, has been styled the highest and finest character among the author's creations. He is most effective in the rôle of campaign manager, whereby he gains the victory for his friend; but his powers are also utilized to bring about the restoration of peace in the Colonel's disrupted household. The brilliant Adelheid, a fitting mate for Bolz and his equal in strength, is an admirable embodiment of the charms and virtues of an upper class, cultured woman. The minor characters are types of their particular stations in life and are flawlessly delineated. The whole is one of the best comedies that the nineteenth century brought forth, and is one of the established pieces of the German theatres.

The translator has endeavored to give to the student an aid in properly and idiomatically reproducing in English this model of colloquial German, making it as literal as is consistent with smoothness and true translation. She will also be much gratified if her efforts are the means of introducing Freytag's masterpiece to some who are deprived of the pleasure of reading it in the original. It should be of especial interest to the people of a democracy, for it is directly based on the burgher

6   THE JOURNALISTS

principles for which a democracy stands,
and of which Freytag was so ardent an
advocate.

THE JOURNALISTS

CAST OF CHARACTERS

Colonel Berg, retired.
Ida, his daughter.
Adelheid Runeck.
Senden, a squire.
Professor Oldendorf, editor ⎤
Konrad Bolz, editor
Bellmaus, associate editor   of the
Kämpe, associate editor   ⎬ newspaper
Körner, associate editor   *Union.*
Henning, publisher and owner
Müller, office boy ⎦

Schmock, associate editor ⎤   of the
                    ⎬ newspaper
Blumenberg, editor   ⎦ *Coriolanus.*
Piepenbrink, wine dealer and voter.
Lotte, his wife.
Bertha, their daughter.
Kleinmichel, citizen and voter.
Fritz, his son.
Schwarz, counsellor-at-law.
A strange dancer.
Korb, secretary of Adelheid's estate.
Karl, servant of the Colonel.
A waiter.
Guests of the club. Committees of citizens.
    SCENE: *The capital of a province.*

FIRST ACT

FIRST SCENE

(A large room in the Colonel's house, opening onto a garden. Elaborate furnishings. At centre back, an open door; behind it a veranda and the garden; on either side, large windows. Right and left, doors. Right of immediate foreground, a window. Tables, chairs, a small sofa.

Ida sits in foreground, right, reading a book. Colonel enters through centre door, in his hand an open box in which are dahlias.)

Col. Here, Ida, are the new species of dahlias, which our gardener has raised. You are to find names for them. Think now! Day after to-morrow is the session of the Horticultural Union, and I wish to display our new varieties and to announce their appellations.

Ida. This light-colored one here shall be called "Adelheid."

Col. "Adelheid Runeck"—to be sure! Your own name is not to be used, for you have already been in the flower trade as a dahlia a long time.

9

Ida. One shall be named after your favorite author, ''Boz.''

Col. Fine! And it must be a right splendid one, too—here—this yellow one with the violet tips. And the third—what shall we christen this one?

Ida. (*Pleadingly extending her hand to her father.*) ''Eduard Oldendorf.''

Col. What? The Professor? The editor? No, that won't do! It was bad enough when he took over the paper; but I can never forgive his allowing himself to be misled by his party into being a candidate for the Chamber.

Ida. There he comes, now!

Col. (*Aside.*) It used to be a pleasure to me to hear his footstep. Now I have to watch myself, lest I become discourteous whenever I see him.

(*Enter Oldendorf.*)

Old. Good morning, Colonel.

Ida. (*Cordially.*) Good morning, Oldendorf. Help me look over the new dahlias that my father has raised.

Col. Do not annoy the Professor. Such trifles are nothing to him any more. He is interested in greater things.

Old. At any rate, I have not become incapable of enjoying that which gives you pleasure.

Col. (*Muttering to himself.*) You

haven't proved that to me exactly! I feared you enjoyed doing that which vexed me. You have a great deal to do now, of course, with your election, Mr. Would-be-Member?

Old. You know, Colonel, that I myself have the least to do with it.

Col. Oh, but I think you have! Generally, in such elections, you know, it is the custom to pay court to influential persons, to press the voters' hands, to deliver speeches, to scatter promises on all sides, and to carry on all those disreputable practices, whatever you may call them.

Old. But, Colonel, you surely do not believe that I will do anything unworthy?

Col. No? I am not sure, Oldendorf. Since you have become a journalist, since you have been editing your *Union,* and every day have been reproaching the government with how faultily it is managed, since that time you are no longer as of old.

Old. (*Who, up to this time, has been examining the flowers with Ida, turning to the Col.*) Does what I now say or write contradict my earlier views? You will scarcely be able to prove that to me, and even less that you have noticed any change in my feelings and conduct towards you.

Col. (*Obdurately.*) Well, really, that *would* be very fine! I will not waste the

morning in argument. Ida may see whether
she can get along better with you. I am going to my flowers. (*Takes box and exits
towards garden.*)

Old. Whence comes the bad humor of
your father? Has something from the
newspaper irritated him again?

Ida. I think not. It does grieve him,
however, to have you in a position in politics to advocate measures which he hates,
and to attack policies which he venerates.
(*Shyly.*) Oldendorf, is it then impossible
for you to withdraw from the campaign?

Old. It is impossible.

Ida. I would justify you here and my
father could recover his good nature, for
he would appreciate very highly the sacrifice which you would be making for him.
Then we might hope that our future would
be as peaceful as the past has been.

Old. I know that, Ida, and the prospect
of becoming the representative of this city
gives me every feeling except joy, yet I cannot withdraw.

Ida. (*Turning away.*) My father is
right. Since you have been editing the
paper you have become another man.

Old. Ida! You, too? If this discord
comes between us two, then I am poor indeed!

Ida. Dear Eduard! I am sad only be-

cause I am to be separated from you for
so long.

Old. But I am not elected yet. If I
become the representative, and things go
as I wish, I shall take you to the capital,
never to let you from my side again.

Ida. Ah, Eduard, we must not think of
that now. Only spare my father.

Old. You see, I endure much from him;
but I do not give up hope that he may
become reconciled to me. When this election is past, then, once more, I will appeal
to him. Perhaps I shall win a gracious decision and our union.

Ida. Just be attentive to his little hób-
bies. He is in the garden, by his dahlia
bed. Admire the gay colors. If you are
very tactful, perhaps he will yet name one
"Eduard Oldendorf." We have already
considered it. Come! (*Exeunt both.*)

(*Enter Senden, Blumenberg, Karl, and
Schmock.*)

Send. (*Entering.*) Is the Colonel
alone?

Karl. Prof. Oldendorf is with him.

Send. Announce us. (*Exit Karl.*) Always and forever this Oldendorf! Listen,
Blumenberg, this relation of the old man
with the *Union* must end. He does not belong to us completely as long as the Profes-

sor has the run of this house. We need the
Colonel's very influential personage——

Blum. And his house is the first in the
city, the best company, good wine and art.

Send. Besides, I have private reasons
for winning over the Colonel to us. And
the Professor and his crowd stand in our
way everywhere.

Blum. The friendship will come to an
end. I promise you that it will end gradually during these weeks. The first step
towards it is already taken. The owners of
the *Union* have fallen into the trap.

Send. What trap?

Blum. The one I set for them in our
paper. (*Turning to Schmock, who is
standing by the door.*) Why are you
standing here, Schmock? Can't you wait
at the gate?

Schmock. I only went where you went.
Why can't I stand here? I know the Colonel as well as you do.

Blum. Don't be impudent, don't be in-
solent! Go and wait at the gate, and if I
bring the article to you, then run straight
to the printing office with it. Do you understand?

Schmock. Why shouldn't I understand
when you screech like a raven? (*Exits.*)

Blum. (*To Send.*) He is a common
person, but he is useful. Now that we are

alone, listen! When you brought me here recently, I begged and urged the Colonel to write down his ideas about the current happenings.

Send. Yes, and I am sorry you did. You flattered him grossly enough, but the old man fired up anyhow.

Blum. We asked him to read aloud what he had written; he read it, we praised it.

Send. It was very tedious, though.

Blum. I begged it from him for our paper.

Send. Unfortunately! And I have to keep carrying bulky articles to your print shop. These essays are too labored. They are no advantage to the *Coriolanus.*

Blum. Yet I have printed them with satisfaction. If one has written for a sheet, he will naturally be a good friend of that sheet. The Colonel immediately subscribed for the *Coriolanus,* and the day after invited me to dine.

Send. (*Shrugging his shoulders.*)   If *that* is the whole advantage!

Blum. It is only the beginning. The articles are stupid. Why shall I not say it?

Send. God knows they are!

Blum. And no one knows who the author is.

Send. The old man demanded that. I believe he is afraid of Oldendorf.

Blum. For that very reason things have come about as I expected. Oldendorf's paper to-day attacked these articles. Here is the latest number of the *Union*.

Send. Show it to me. That will cause a capital misunderstanding. Is the attack harsh?

Blum. The Colonel will certainly consider it harsh. Do you believe that it will help us against the Professor?

Send. On my honor, you are the slyest devil that ever crept out of an inkwell!

Blum. Give that here. The Colonel is coming.

(*Enter the Col.*)

Col. Good   m o r n i n g,   gentlemen! (*Aside.*) And Oldendorf is here now, too! If he will only stay in the garden! Now, Mr. Editor, what is the *Coriolanus* doing?

Blum. Our readers are admiring the new articles signed with the arrow. May I hope—perhaps—something more——

Col. (*Drawing a manuscript from his pocket, looking around.*) I rely upon your discretion. I would really like to read it through once, though, to make sure of the construction of the sentences.

Blum. That can be done most conveniently when the proof is read.

Col. I guess it will pass. Take it, but keep it quiet.

Blum. Permit me to send it to the office immediately. (*At the door.*) Schmock! (*Schmock appears at the door, takes the manuscript, and exits quickly.*)

Send. Blumenberg manages the paper skilfully, but he has enemies. He has to defend himself vigorously.

Col. (*Pleased.*) Enemies? Who does not have them? But you journalists are as nervous as women. Everything arouses you, each word that any one says against you makes you indignant! Go to, but you are sensitive people!

Blum. Perhaps you are right, Colonel. But if one has opponents, like this *Union*——

Col. Yes, the *Union*—that is a thorn in the flesh to you both. There is a great deal in it that I don't like, but this much is true —on the aggressive, especially in sounding the alarm, and in the charge, it is more expert than your sheet. Their articles are witty. Even if they are all wrong, one is obliged to laugh over them.

Blum. Not always. I see no wit at all in to-day's attack on the best articles which the *Coriolanus* has brought out in a long time.

Col. Attack on what articles?

Blum. Upon your own, Colonel. 1 surely must have the paper with me. (*Hunts for it and finally gives him a copy of the "Union."*)

Col. Oldendorf's paper is attacking my essays! (*Reads.*) "We deplore such ignorance——"

Blum. And here——

Col. "It is inexcusable presumption—" What! I was presuming?

Blum. And here——

Col. "One is in doubt whether to call the naïveté of the correspondent laughable or sad. In any case, he has no right to speak with—" (*Throwing the sheet away.*) Oh, that is contemptible! That is abusive! (*Ida and Oldendorf enter from the garden.*)

Send. Now the storm will break!

Col. Professor, your paper is making progress. In addition to poor principles, now comes something else—abuse!

Ida. (*Frightened.*) Father!

Old. (*Stepping forward.*) Colonel, what justifies you in saying these insulting words?

Col. (*Extending the paper to him.*) Look there! *That* stands in your paper, in *your* paper, Oldendorf!

Old. The manner of the attack is not quite as quiet as I would have wished——

Col. (*Interrupting him.*) Not quite as quiet? Really not?

Old. In the matter itself, the attack is correct.

Col. Sir, you dare say that to me!

Ida. Father!

Old. Colonel, I do not comprehend this mood, and I beg you to take into consideration the fact that we speak before witnesses.

Col. Do not ask for any consideration. It would be more fitting for you to show a little consideration for the man to whose friendship you were wont to lay such great claim.

Old. Have the candor to tell me, before every one, what connection you have with these articles in the *Coriolanus* which have been assailed.

Col. A very casual connection, which in your eyes is too insignificant to deserve attention. I am the author of the articles.

Ida. Great heavens!

Old. (*Angrily.*) You? Articles in this man's paper?

Ida. (*Entreatingly.*) Oldendorf!

Old. (*More quietly.*) The *Union* has not attacked *you*, but an unknown writer. who meant nothing to us but a partisan of this gentleman. You might have spared us both this painful scene, if you had not

kept secret from me the fact that you were
a correspondent of the *Coriolanus.*

Col. Henceforth, also, you will have to
endure being left out of my confidence regarding my affairs. You have given me,
here, a printed evidence of friendship
which does not make me long for another.

Old. (*Taking up his hat.*) And I can
only explain to you that, deeply as I deplore the circumstance, I feel that I am
free of all blame. I hope, Colonel, that,
upon quieter reflection, you will arrive at
the same conclusion. Farewell, Fräulein. I
commend myself to you. (*Goes as far as
the centre door.*)

Ida. (*Beseechingly.*) Father, do not
let him leave us in this way!

Col. It is better than if he should remain.

(*Enter Adelheid.*)

Adel. (*Entering in an elegant travel-
ling costume, meets Oldendorf at the
door.*) Not so fast, Professor!

Old. (*Kisses her hand and exits.*)

| *Ida.* | | Adelheid! (*Hastens into her arms.*) Adel- |
| *Col.* | (*Together.*) | heid! And r i g h t now, at the right mo- ment! |

Adel. (*Embracing Ida, extending her
hand to the Colonel.*) Shake hands with

your country cousin! My aunt sends
greetings and the estate of Rosenau, in its
brown autumn garb, humbly presents its
compliments. The fields are bare and the
dry foliage in the garden dances in the
wind. Ah, Herr von Senden!

Col. (*Introducing.*)   The editor, Herr
Blumenberg.

Send. We are charmed to greet our en-
ergetic agriculturist in the city.

Adel. And we would have rejoiced to
meet our next door neighbor in the country.

Col. He has much to do here. He is
a great politician and labors zealously for
the good cause.

Adel. Yes, yes, we read of his doings
in the paper. Yesterday I drove over your
farm. Your overseer has not yet finished
harvesting your potato crop.

Send. The Rosenau people have the
privilege of being through a week earlier
than any one else.

Adel. For that very reason we understand nothing but our farming. (*Friendly.*)
The neighborhood sends its greetings.

Send. Thank you. We will now yield
you to your friends, who have stronger
claims on you, but grant me an interview
to-day, so that I may learn the news from
our region.

Adel. (*Bows.*)

Send. Farewell, Colonel. (*To Ida.*) I commend myself to your favor, Fräulein. (*Exits with Blumenberg.*)

Ida. (*Embracing Adel.*) I have you! Now everything will be well.

Adel. What is to be well? Is there something wrong? Back there some one passed me more quickly than is his usual custom—and here I see wet eyes and a clouded brow. (*Kisses her on the eyes.*) They must not spoil your pretty eyes. And you, my worthy friend, show me a pleasant face.

Col. You will remain with us through the winter, won't you? It is the first you have given us in a long time. We shall seek to deserve this honor.

Adel. (*Soberly.*) It is the first time, since my father's death, that I have had any desire to mingle with the world again. Besides, I have business here. You know, I came of age this summer, and our legal friend, Justizrat Schwarz, demands my presence. Listen, Ida, the servants are unpacking. Go and see that they do it properly. (*Aside.*) And put a wet cloth over your eyes. One can see that you have been weeping. (*Ida exits right. Adel. steps quickly to the Col.*) What is wrong between Ida and the Professor?

Col. It is a long story. I do not wish
to spoil my pleasure now. Things are not
well with us men. Our views are so different.

Adel. Were not your views different
formerly, too? And yet your relation with
Oldendorf was so pleasant.

Col. They were not as different as they
are now.

Adel. And which of you has changed?

Col. Hm! He, to be sure. He is mis-
guided in much by his bad surroundings.
There are several people, journalists on his
paper; above all others, a certain Bolz.

Adel. (*Aside.*) What am I to hear?

Col. But you know him well yourself, of
course. He comes from your vicinity.

Adel. He was a Rosenau child.

Col. I remember. Your sainted father,
my revered General, could not bear him,
either.

Adel. At least, he has said that, at
times.

Col. Since then, this Bolz has become
a queer fellow. He must needs live in a
free and easy way, and his customs seem
to be somewhat loose. He is Oldendorf's
evil genius.

Adel. That would be sad! No, I do not
believe that.

Col. What don't you believe, Adelheid?

Adel. I do not believe in evil spirits.
Whatever is wrong between you and Oldendorf can be made right again. To-day,
enemy; to-morrow, friend. So it goes in
politics; but Ida's feelings will not change
so quickly. Colonel, I have brought with
me some beautiful new material for a gown.
I intend to wear the gown this winter as a
bridesmaid.

Col. That is not to be thought of! I
will not let myself be caught in that way,
girl. I shall carry the war into the enemy's
country. Why do you keep driving other
people to the altar and yet, yourself, cause
the whole neighborhood to jokingly call you
the "Sleeping Beauty" and the maiden
farmer?

Adel. (*Laughing.*) Yes, that is what
they call me.

Col. The richest heiress of the entire
region, surrounded by an army of suitors,
and yet so impervious to sentiment! No
one can explain that.

Adel. My dear Colonel, if our young
men were as admirable as certain older
ones—ah! but they are not.

Col. You shall not evade me. We will
keep you in the city until, among our young
men, one is found whom you consider
worthy to march under your command;
for whomever you choose for a husband, in

the end it will fare with him as with me—
he will have to act according to your de-
sires.

Adel. (*Quickly.*) Will you act according to my desire with Ida and Professor
Oldendorf? Now I have you cornered.

Col. Will you do me the favor of making your choice of a husband here with us
this winter? Yes? Now, I have caught
you!

Adel. It is a bargain! Shake on it!
(*Holds out her hand to him.*)

Col. (*Shakes it and laughs.*) There
you were outwitted! (*Exits through the
middle door.*)

Adel. (*Alone.*) I think not! So, Herr
Konrad Bolz, that is' your reputation
among the people? You live in a free and
easy way? You have loose customs? You
are an evil genius?

(*Enter Korb.*)

Korb. (*From centre door, with a pack-
age.*) Where shall I carry the account
books and papers, gracious lady?

Adel. Into my room. Listen, dear Korb
—did you find your room in order?

Korb. In the most beautiful order. The
servant put in two stearin candles for me
to use. It is sheer extravagance.

Adel. You are not to touch a pen for me
the whole day long. I wish you to look

around the city and call on your acquaintances. You have acquaintances here, of course?

Korb. Not so very many. It is over a year since I have been here.

Adel. (*Indifferently.*) Are there any Rosenau people here?

Korb. Among the soldiers there are four from the village. There is Johann Lutz von Schimmellutz——

Adel. I know. Is there no one else here from the village whom you know?

Korb. No one else, except him, of course——

Adel. Except *him?* Who is that?

Korb. Why, our Herr Konrad.

Adel. To be sure. He *is* here. Won't you call upon him? I believe you have always been good friends.

Korb. Will I call upon him? My first call will be on him. During the whole journey I was rejoicing at the prospect. He is a true soul, of whom the village may well be proud.

Adel. (*Warmly.*) Yes, he has a true heart.

Korb. (*Enthusiastically.*) Always merry and friendly, and how attached he is to the village! The poor man! He has not been there for so long.

Adel. Not a word about that!

Korb. He will ask me all sorts of questions—about the farm——

Adel. (*Excitedly.*) And about the horses. The old dun, on which he liked to ride, is still living.

Korb. And about the bushes which he planted with you.

Adel. Especially the lilac bush, where my arbor now stands. Tell him about that.

Korb. And about the pond. Sixty times threescore carp——

Adel. And threescore golden tench—do not forget that. And the old carp, with the copper ring which he put around his body, was pulled out with the rest at the last haul, but we put him back in again.

Korb. And how he will question me about you, Fräulein!

Adel. Tell him that I am well.

Korb. And how you have run the estate since the General's death; and how you take his paper, which I read aloud afterwards to the farmers.

Adel. You do not need to tell him that, exactly. (*Aside, sighing.*) I won't find out anything in this way. (*Pause, then with earnestness.*) Listen, Korb, my friend. I have heard many things about Herr Bolz which have amazed me. He is said to be wild.

Korb. Yes, I believe that. He was always a wild young colt.

Adel. He is supposed to spend more money than he takes in.

Korb. Yes, that is quite possible. But he spends it gaily; of that I am convinced.

Adel. (*Aside.*) I won't get any consolation from him! (*Indifferently.*) He, no doubt, has a good position now. I wonder if he will not soon be looking for a wife.

Korb. A wife? No, he won't do that; that is not possible.

Adel. I have certainly heard something to that effect. At least, he is supposed to be much interested in a young lady. People are talking of it.

Korb. That would surely be——. No, I don't believe it! (*Hastily.*) I will ask him about that the first thing.

Adel. He himself will be the last person to tell you. Such a thing is ascertained from the friends and acquaintances of a man. The people in the village should know if he is to marry a Rosenau girl.

Korb. Certainly. I must find out about it.

Adel. You will have to be very clever to do it. You know how sharp he is.

Korb. Oh, you'll see that I'll outwit him. I shall manage it!

Adel. Go, good Korb. (*Exit Korb.*)

That was sad news that the Colonel gave
me. Konrad profligate, unworthy! It is
impossible! A noble mind cannot be so
changed. I do not believe a word of all
that they tell me about him. (*Exits.*)

(Editorial room of the *Union.* Doors at
centre and both sides. In foreground, left,
a work table with journals and papers.
Right, a similar, smaller table. Chairs.
Bolz calls from the side door, right, at
which Müller enters, centre.)
Bolz. (*Impatiently.*) Müller! Man-of-
all-work! Where is the mail?
Müller. (*Enters briskly with a bundle
of letters and newspapers.*) Here, Herr
Bolz, is the mail—and here, from the printer's, is the proof sheet of this evening's
issue for revision.
Bolz. (*Quickly opening the letters at
table, left, reading them through and mark-
ing them with pencil.*) I have already
made the revision, you old rascal.
Müller. Not entirely. There is still the
miscellaneous column, which Herr Bellmaus has given to the typesetters.
Bolz. Give it to me. (*Reads.*) ''Washing Stolen from the Ground—Triplets Born

—Concert, Concert—Society Session—
Theatre"—everything all right—"Recently Invented Locomotive—The Great Sea-
serpent Sighted." (*Springing up.*) Great
heavens! There he comes again with that
old sea-serpent! I wish that it were cooked
to a jelly for him, and that he would be
forced to eat it up, cold. (*Hurries to door
at right.*) Bellmaus, monster, come here!
(*Enter Bellmaus.*)

Bell. (*Coming in from right, pen in
hand.*) What is the matter? Why the
noise?

Bolz. (*Solemnly.*) Bellmaus, when we
did you the honor to entrust to you the
preparation of the miscellaneous matter for
this sheet, it was not the intention that you
should waltz the everlasting great sea-serpent through the columns of our paper!
How could you put in that threadbare lie
again?

Bell. It just fitted. We lacked six lines.

Bolz. That is an excuse, but not a good
one. Hunt out your own stories—what are
you a journalist for? Make a little "Special Correspondence"—for example, a dis-
sertation on "Human Life in General," or
on the "Dogs Running About the Street,"
or look up some blood-curdling story, perhaps an assassination, according to the
code, or how a hamster has bitten to death

seven children, or some such thing. There is so much that happens, and so tremendously much that doesn't happen that a self-respecting newspaper correspondent should never lack for news.

Bell. Give it here; I'll change it. (*Goes to the table, looks in a printed sheet, cuts a clipping from it with a large pair of shears and pastes it on the issue of the newspaper.*)

Bolz. Quite right, my son. Do that and better yourself. (*Opening the door, right.*) Kämpe, can you come in for a moment? (*To Müller, who is waiting at the door.*) Away with the revision to the printery! (*Müller takes the sheet from Bellmaus, hastens out.*)

(*Enter Kämpe.*)

Kämpe. (*Entering.*) I certainly cannot write anything decent when you are making such a noise.

Bolz. So? What have you been writing now? Doubtless, at the most, a love letter to a ballet-girl, or an order to your tailor?

Bell. No, he is writing tender letters. He is seriously in love, for yesterday he took me walking in the moonlight and spoke contemptuously of all dissipations.

Kämpe. (*Who has seated himself comfortably.*) Gentlemen, it is unfair to call a man away from his work to make such poor jokes.

Bolz. Yes, yes. He slanders you openly in asserting that you love anything except your new boots—and your own person a very little bit. You are of an exuberantly loving disposition yourself, little Bellmaus. You glow like a pastille as often as you see a young lady. You flutter around, smouldering and smoking, and yet, after all, you don't have the courage to address her once; but one must make allowances for him. He is by nature a lyric poet, and therefore he is shy. He blushes before the ladies and still is capable of beautiful emotions.

Bell. I do not wish to let my poetry be thrown in my teeth, unheard. Did I ever read it to you?

Bolz. No, thank Heaven! You never had the impudence. (*Seriously.*) But to the business at hand, gentlemen! To-day's issue is ready. Oldendorf is not here yet, so let us have a private conference meanwhile. Oldendorf *must* be in the next Chamber as deputy from this city—our party and the *Union* must put that through. How do our chances stand to-day?

Kämpe. As good as possible. Our opponents admit that no other candidate would be as dangerous to them, and our friends, everywhere, have the highest hopes, but you know how little that signifies. Here is the list of the voters. Our committee sends word to you that our estimates were correct. Of the hundred voters of our city, forty, with certainty, belong to us. Approximately as many more stand on the lists of the opposing party; the remaining twenty votes are uncertain. It is clear that the election will depend upon a very small majority.

Bolz. And we, naturally, shall have the majority, a majority of from eight to ten votes. You can count upon that with the greatest safety. Many a one who is as yet undecided will come to us when he hears that we are the stronger. Where is the list of the uncertain voters? (*Looks on.*)

Kämpe. I have marked those who, in the opinion of our friends, would be open to influence.

Bolz. By this name I see two crosses. What do they mean?

Kämpe. That is Piepenbrink, the wine seller Piepenbrink. He has a large following in his district, is a well-to-do man, and is said to control more than five or six of the votes of his adherents.

Bolz. We must have *him!* What sort of a man is he?

Kämpe. He is supposed to be very

rough and not to trouble himself over politics at all.

Bell. He has a pretty daughter, though.

Kämpe. Of what use is his pretty daughter? I would prefer that he had an ugly wife, then it would be easier to get at him.

Bell. That he has also—a woman with scanty locks and fire-red ribbons on her cap.

Bolz. With or without a wife, the man must be ours. Be still! Some one is coming. That is Oldendorf's step. He must know nothing of our deliberations. Go to your rooms, gentlemen. This evening we will continue.

Kämpe. (*At the door.*) It is still understood, then, that in the next issue I attack the *Coriolanus'* new correspondent again, the one with the arrow?

Bolz. Of course. Attack him in a dignified way, but make it vigorous. A little struggle with our opponents before the voters just now will be effective, and the "arrow" articles offer some very weak spots.

(*Exeunt Kämpe and Bellmaus.*)

(*Enter Oldendorf, centre.*)

Old. Good-day, Konrad.

Bolz. (*At the table, right, looking over the election lists.*) Blessed be your arrival!

There lies the correspondence. There is
nothing of importance.

Old. Do you need me here to-day?

Bolz. No, darling. The evening edition
is ready and Kämpe is writing the chief
editorial for to-morrow.

Old. About what?

Bolz. A little skirmish with the *Coriolanus* again. Against the unknown correspondent with the arrow who has attacked
our party. But don't be alarmed. I have
told Kämpe that he is to keep the article
dignified, very dignified.

Old. The article must not be written!
Not for the world!

Bolz. I do not understand you. Why
does one have political opponents if he may
not attack them?

Old. Just listen. These articles are written by the Colonel. He told me so to-day,
himself.

Bolz. Good heavens!

Old. (*Darkly.*) You can imagine that
this admission was accompanied by intima-
tions which make my relations with the
Colonel and his household rather strained
just now.

Bolz. (*Earnestly.*) And what does the
Colonel demand of you?

Old. He will be reconciled to me, if I

resign the editorship of the paper and re-
nounce my candidacy.

Bolz. The devil! He doesn't want much!

Old. I suffer amidst this discord. To
you, my friend, I can say that.

Bolz. (*Stepping up to him and pressing his hand.*) Solemn moment of manly
emotion!

Old. Don't play the clown now, of all
times. You can imagine how painful my
position in the Colonel's house has become.
The worthy old man either cold or furious,
the conversation spiced with biting insin-
uations, Ida suffering. I often see that she
has been weeping. If our party wins and
I become the representative from this city,
then I fear that every hope of a union with
Ida will be taken away from me.

Bolz. (*Warmly.*) And if you withdraw
our party will suffer a decided loss. (*Rapidly and emphatically.*) The approaching
session of the Chamber will be a momentous
one for the state. The parties are nearly
equal. Every loss of a vote is a detriment
to our cause. In this city we have no candidate besides yourself whose popularity
is great enough to assure his election. If
you step out of the contest for any reason
whatsoever, our adversaries win.

Old. Unfortunately, it is as you say.

Bolz. (*More and more earnestly.*) I

will not speak of the confidence that I place
in your ability. I am convinced that you
will be in the Chamber and perhaps serve
your country as a member of the ministry.
I beg you, now, to think only of the duties
which you have assumed towards our political friends who trust you and towards
this paper and us, who have worked assidu-
ously for three years to bring the name of
Oldendorf, which stands at the top of the
sheet, into prominence. It is a question of
your honor, and each moment of hesitancy
would be an injustice in you.

Old. (*With dignity.*) You are becoming excited without occasion. Even I would
consider it wrong to draw back now, when
I am told that I am necessary to our cause;
but if I confess to you, my friend, that the
decision is made at great cost to me, I do
not thereby compromise either our cause or
us two.

Bolz. (*Conciliatingly.*) You are quite
right. You are an honorable comrade.
And so, peace, friendship, courage! Your
old Colonel will not be implacable.

Old. He has become intimate with Senden, who flatters him on all sides, and, as I
feared, has plans which touch me closely,
also. I would be still more uneasy if I did
not know that just now I have a good ally

in the Colonel's house. Adelheid Runeck
has just arrived.

Bolz. Adelheid Runeck? She here too!
(*Calling quickly through the door at
right.*) Kämpe, the article against the
knight of the arrow is *not* written. Do you
understand?

Kämpe. (*At the door, pen in hand.*)
What is to be written, then?

Bolz. Hanged if I know! Listen. Perhaps I can induce Oldendorf to write to-
morrow's editorial himself; but, in any
case, you must have something ready.

Kämpe. But what?

Bolz. (*Sharply.*)   Write about the emi-
gration to Australia, for all I care—that
won't cause any offence, at any rate.

Kämpe. Good! Am I to advocate it, or
advise against it?

Bolz. (*Sharply.*)   Advise against it,
naturally. We need all the people who are
willing to work here with us in this country. Picture Australia as a miserable hole
—truthful throughout, but as black as possible. How the kangaroo, rolled up in a
ball, springs at the head of the settler with
incredible malice, while the duck-bill is
pinching him in the back of his legs; how
the gold prospector in the winter has to
stand in salt water up to his neck, while
through three months of the summer he has

not one swallow to drink; and if he survives all this, he is at last eaten up by thievish natives. Make it right vivid, and at the end put the latest market price of Australian wool out of the *London Times*. You will find the necessary books in the library. (*Slams the door.*)

Old. (*At the table.*) Do you know Fräulein Runeck? She frequently asks after you in her letters to Ida.

Bolz. So? Yes, I know her, to be sure. We are from the same village; she from the manor house, I from the parsonage. My father used to teach us together. Oh, yes, I know her.

Old. How does it come that you have become such strangers to each other? You never speak of her.

Bolz. Hm! It is the old story—family feuds—Montagues and Capulets! I have not seen her for a long time.

Old. (*Smiling.*) I hope politics did not estrange you.

Bolz. Politics, I must admit, were involved in our separation to a certain extent. You see, it is a common misfortune for friendship to be broken up through partisanship.

Old. It is sad. In matters of faith every educated man will tolerate the convictions of his fellows; and in politics we

treat each other like reprobates because the
one differs by a few shades from his neighbor.

Bolz. (*Aside.*) Material for the next
editorial! (*Aloud.*) Differs from his
neighbor. My idea, exactly. That must be
put into our sheet. (*Beseechingly.*) Listen—just a little moral article—admoni-
tion to our voters—respect for our rivals!
For they are, after all, our brothers! (*More
and more beseechingly.*) Oldendorf, that
would be just the thing for you. In that
theme there is virtue and humanity. The
writing will divert you and you owe the
paper an article on account of forbidding
the combat. Do me the favor! Write
there in the back room. No one shall disturb you.

Old. (*Smiling.*) You are a base in-
triguer!

Bolz. (*Forcing him from his chair.*)
Please! You will find paper and ink there.
Come! my treasure, come! (*Leads him to the
door, left. Oldendorf exits. Bolz calls in.*)
Will you have a cigar? An old "Ugues?"
(*Takes a cigar case from his pocket.*)
No? Do not write too little! It is to
be the leading editorial. (*Closes the door;
calls through door, right.*) The Professor
is writing the article himself. Take care
that no one disturbs him. (*Advancing to

foreground.) That is settled, I trust. Adelheid here in the city! Then I will go to her immediately! Hold on! Just keep cool! You, my old Bolz, are no longer the brown youngster from the parsonage garden, and even if you were, *she* has become a stranger long since. The grass has grown over the grave of a certain childish affection. Why are you thumping so restlessly, my dear heart? She is just as far removed from you here in the city as upon her estate. (*Seating himself, playing with a pencil.*) "Nothing like keeping cool!" muttered the salamander as he sat down in the oven fire.

(Enter Korb.)

Korb. Is Herr Bolz to be found here?

Bolz. (*Springing up.*) Korb! Dear Korb! Welcome, heartily welcome! It is fine that you have not forgotten me! (*Shaking his hand.*) I am rejoiced to see you.

Korb. And I much more! Well, here we are in the city! The whole village sends greetings! From Anton, the stableboy— he is foreman now—to the old night watchman whose horn you hung on the top of the tower in those days. Oh, but I am glad to see you!

Bolz. How goes it with the young lady? Tell me, old man.

Korb. Splendidly, now. But things have been bad. The late General was ill four years and that was a hard time. You know he was always an irritable man.

Bolz. Yes, he *was* difficult to handle.

Korb. And especially so during his sickness; but the young lady nursed him as tenderly as a lamb, and at the last, as pale. Now, since he is dead, she carries on the farming alone, and like the best of managers. There is prosperity in the village now. I shall tell you everything, but not until this evening. The young lady is waiting for me. I just ran down here for a moment to tell you we are here.

Bolz. Not so fast, Korb. So the people in the village still think of me?

Korb. I should say so. No one can explain to himself why you do not come to see us. As long as the old man was living it was somewhat different, but now——

Bolz. (*Seriously.*) My parents are dead. A stranger is living in the parsonage.

Korb. But we at the manor house are still alive! The mistress would surely be glad.

Bolz. Does she remember me yet?

Korb. Certainly. She asked after you only to-day.

Bolz. What about, old man?

Korb. She asked me if what people are saying were true, that you had become a wild fellow, were contracting debts, flirting and cutting up generally.

Bolz. Oh, woe! Did you vindicate me?

Korb. That is understood. I told her that all that was to be expected from you.

Bolz. The deuce you did! She thinks of me in that way? Listen, Korb, Fräulein Adelheid has many suitors, I suppose?

Korb. The sand by the sea is nothing in comparison.

Bolz. (*Irritatedly.*) She can finally choose but one, at any rate.

Korb. (*Craftily.*) Correct! But whom? That is the question.

Bolz. Whom do you think?

Korb. Well, that is hard to say. There is this Herr von Senden, who is living in the city now. If any one has prospects it surely is he. He is as busy as a weasel around us. Just now, as I was leaving the house, he sent there a full dozen cards of admission to the club reception. It must be a queer sort of club, where the upper classes mingle intimately with the burghers.

Bolz. Yes, it is a political organization, in which Senden is director. It is fishing for votes on a large scale. And the Colonel and the ladies are going?

Korb. So I hear. Even I have received a ticket.

Bolz. (*To himself.*) Has it come to this? Poor Oldendorf! And Adelheid at Herr von Senden's club reception!

Korb. (*To himself.*) How shall I set about getting next to his love affairs? (*Aloud.*) By the way, Konrad, one thing more. Do you happen to have, in this house, a right good friend, to whom you could recommend me?

Bolz. What for, old fellow?

Korb. It is only—I am a stranger in the place, and many times I have errands and commissions, in which I don't know what to do. So I would like to have some one here from whom I could get my information if, at any time, you are absent, or with whom I could leave anything for you.

Bolz. You will find me here nearly the whole day. (*At the door.*) Bellmaus!
(*Enter Bellmaus.*)
See this gentleman here. He is a good old friend of mine, from my home town. If, some time, he should not find me in then you are to take my place. This gentleman's name is Bellmaus and he is a good fellow.

Korb. I am glad to make your acquaintance, Herr Bellmaus.

Bell. I, as well, Herr—. You have not told me the name.

Bolz. Korb! Basket! Of the great family of market baskets! He has had much to carry in his life. He has often even carried me on his shoulders.

Bell. I am delighted, Herr Korb. (*They shake each other's hands.*)

Korb. So—settled. And now I must go, or the Fräulein will be waiting.

Bolz. Good-by. See you again soon. (*Exit Korb. Bellmaus exits through door at right.*)

Bolz. (*Alone.*) So this Senden is courting her. Oh, that is bitter!

(*Enter Henning, followed by Müller.*)

Henn. (*In dressing gown, hastily, a printed sheet in his hand.*) Servant, Herr Bolz! Is it K-o-n-d-i-t-o-r, or K-a-n-d-i-t-o-r? The new proof reader corrected K-a-n-d-i-t-o-r.

Bolz. (*Absorbed in thought.*) My valiant Herr Henning, the *Union* prints it Konditor.

Henn. I said so at once. (*To Müller.*) It must be changed. The press is waiting. (*Müller exits hurriedly.*) I have taken this opportunity to read the editorial. It is yours, I judge. It is very good, but too sharp, dear Herr Bolz. Pepper and mustard—that will give offence, that will make bad blood.

Bolz. (*Engrossed, angrily.*) I have always had an antipathy to that man.

Henn. (*Insulted.*) How? What? Herr Bolz! You have an antipathy to me?

Bolz. To whom? No, dear Herr Henning. You are an excellent gentleman and would be the foremost of all newspaper owners, if once in awhile you were not a timid hare. (*Embraces him.*) Give my compliments to Madame Henning, sir, and leave me alone. I am pondering the next article.

Henn. (*While he is being pushed out.*) Just write very gently and kindly, dear Herr Bolz.

Bolz. (*Alone, again pacing around.*) Senden avoids me whenever he can. He endures things from me that would arouse any one else to resentment. Is it possible that he suspects——

(*Enter Müller.*)

Müller. (*Hastily.*) A strange lady wishes to pay her respects.

Bolz. (*Quickly.*) A lady? To see me?

Müller. The editor. (*Gives him a card.*)

Bolz. (*Reads.*) ''Leontine Pavoni-Gessler, née Melloni, from Paris.'' She must be an actress. Is she pretty?

Müller. Hm! So-so!

Bolz. Then tell her that we are sorry

that we cannot have the pleasure, but it is
the staff's regular washing day.

Müller. What?

Bolz. (*Angrily.*) Washing, children's
washing. We are sitting in soapsuds up to
the elbows!

Müller. And am I to——

Bolz (*Impatiently.*) You are a block-
head! (*At the door.*) Bellmaus!

(*Enter Bellmaus.*)

Remain here and receive this call.
(*Gives him the card.*)

Bell. Oh, it is the new dancer who is
expected here. (*Examining his coat.*) But
I haven't made any toilette at all.

Bolz. She will have taken pains enough
for both. (*To Müller.*) Let the lady in!
(*Exit Müller.*)

Bell. But I cannot really——

Bolz. (*Angrily.*) To the devil with
your toilette! Don't primp so! (*Goes to
the table, shuts the papers in the drawer,
takes up his hat.*)

(*Enter Madame Pavoni.*)

Mme. Pav. Have I the honor of seeing the editor of the *Union* before me?

Bell. (*Bowing.*) To be sure—that is—
will you not have the goodness to be seated?
(*Pushes up chairs.*)

Bolz. Adelheid is keen-eyed and clever.

How is it possible that she does not see through the fellow?

Mme. Pav. Mr. Editor, the soulful articles on art which adorn your paper have prompted me to——

Bell. Oh, please!

Bolz. (*With decision.*) I must gain admission to this club reception! (*Exits past the lady with a bow. Bellmaus and Mme. Pavoni sit opposite each other. Curtain falls.*)

SECOND ACT

(The Colonel's summer parlor. In the foreground, at right, Ida and Adelheid. Beside Adelheid, the Colonel. All sitting. Before them a table, with a coffee service.)

Col. (*In conversation with Adelheid. Laughing.*) A droll story and splendidly told. I am overjoyed that you are with us, dear Adelheid. Now something besides those wretched politics will be discussed at our table! Hm! The Professor doesn't come to-day. He has never failed us before at afternoon coffee. (*Pause. Ida and Adelheid look at each other. Ida sighs.*)

Adel. Perhaps he has to work.

Ida. Or he is angry at us because I am going to the reception to-night.

Col. Stuff and nonsense! You are not his wife, not even—formally—his fiancée. You are in the house of your father and belong in my circle. Hm! I notice he is resentful towards me since I spoke my mind recently. I believe I was somewhat hasty.

Adel. (*Nodding her head.*) Yes, I hear, somewhat.

49

Ida. He is troubled over your frame of mind, dear father.

Col. Well, I have reason enough to be vexed. Do not remind me of it. And the fact that he is still entangled in this election, that is inexcusable. (*Walks up and down.*) Just send for him, Ida, if you will. (*Ida rings.*)

(*Enter Karl.*)

Ida. Our compliments to the Professor, and tell him we are waiting for him to take coffee with us. (*Exit Karl.*)

Col. Well, it wasn't quite necessary to say "waiting." We have already drunk.

Adel. My Ida hasn't yet.

Ida. Be still!

Adel. Why in the world has he had himself announced as candidate? He has business enough without.

Col. All ambition, girl. The devil of ambition lies in these young men. He drives them as steam does the locomotive.

Ida. No, father, he was not thinking of himself in this matter.

Col. They don't say out bluntly: "I am determined to have a career," or "I *will* be a celebrated man." They're more subtle about it than that. Their good friends come to them and say: "It is your duty to the good cause." "It is a crime against the Fatherland if you don't." "It

is a sacrifice for you, but we demand it.''—
And thus a nice mantle is hung over his
vanity, and the candidate leaps forth—out
of pure patriotism, of course. Do not teach
an old soldier knowledge of the world.
We, dear Adelheid, sit quietly, and laugh
over these foibles.

Adel. And bear them with indulgence,
whenever we have as kind a heart as you.

Col. Yes, experience makes one wise.

(*Enter Karl.*)

Karl. Herr von Senden and two other
men.

Col. What do they want? Very glad to
see them. (*Exit Karl.*) Children, permit
me to bring them in here. Senden never
will stay. His is a restless spirit. (*The
ladies rise.*)

Ida. Our coffee hour is disturbed again.

Adel. Don't fret. We shall have just
that much more time to dress. (*Adel. and
Ida exeunt at left. Enter Senden, Blumenberg, a third gentleman.*)

Send. Colonel, we come on behalf of
the subcommittee for the approaching election, to notify you that the decision, unani-
mously arrived at by the committee, is to
nominate you, Colonel, as the candidate of
our party.

Col. Me?

Send. The committee begs you to give

your consent to this resolution, so that the
necessary announcement may be made to
the voters this evening at the reception.

Col. Do you speak in earnest, my dear
Senden? How did the committee come to
this conclusion?

Send. Colonel, the president who, according to previous arrangement, was to
represent our city, considered it more
profitable to run in a provincial district.
Besides him no one lives in our city who
is so well known and so beloved by the community as you are. If you grant our request, our party is certain of victory. If
you decline, then there is the greatest
probability that the opposition will accomplish their purpose. You will agree with
us that such an outcome must be avoided
under all circumstances.

Col. I perceive all that, but out of personal reasons it is quite impossible for me
to serve our friends in this matter.

Send. (*To the others.*) Permit me to
cite to the Colonel something which will,
perhaps, make him yield to our wishes.
(*Blumenberg and the other gentleman
exeunt into the garden, where they come
into sight occasionally.*)

Col. But, Senden, how could you put
me into this embarrassing situation? You
know that Oldendorf has been intimate in

my house for years, and that it would necessarily be very unpleasant for me to op-
pose him openly.

Send. If the Professor really has such
an attachment for you and your house, he
now has the finest opportunity to show it.
It is self-evident that he will withdraw
immediately.

Col. I am not so sure of that. He is
very stubborn in many things.

Send. If he doesn't withdraw, such
selfishness can scarcely be called stubborn-
ness. And in that case you will hardly
maintain a duty towards him, a duty,
Colonel, which would bring disgrace to the
whole country. Besides, he has no chance
of being elected if you accept. You will defeat him by not a large, but an assured
majority.

Col. Then is our majority certain?

Send. I believe that I am able to vouch
for that. Blumenberg and the other gentleman have made a very careful investi-
gation.

Col. It would serve the Professor just
right, if he was forced to retire on my
account. But, no—no, it won't do, my
friend.

Send. We know, Colonel, what a sacrifice we are demanding of you, and that
nothing can repay you for it, except the

consciousness of having performed a great
service for your country.

Col. To be sure.

Send. That would be respected, even in
the capital, and I am convinced that your
entrance into the Chamber will call forth
great joy in other circles than among your
numerous friends and admirers.

Col. I would meet many old friends
and associates there. (*To himself.*) I
should be presented at court.

Send. Recently the Minister of War
inquired with much cordiality after you.
He must have been an army comrade of
yours.

Col. Surely. We were lively young
chaps in the same company, and committed
many a wild prank together. It would be
a pleasure to me to see how he manages
to draw his honorable countenance into a
solemn frown in the Chamber. He was a
gay devil in the regiment, but an honest
youth.

Send. And he will not be the only one
who will receive you with open arms.

Col. In any case I should have to think
the matter over.

Send. Do not be angry, Colonel, if I
urge you to decide in our favor. This
evening we must present to the summoned

citizens their representative. It is high
time, if all is not to be lost.

Col. (*Uncertainly.*) Senden, you drive
me to the wall. (*Senden beckons the gentlemen to come nearer from the garden
gate.*)

Blum. We dare to press you because we
know that as good a soldier as yourself
arrives at his decisions rapidly.

Col. (*After an inward struggle.*) Well,
so be it, gentlemen. I accept. Say to the
committee that I know how to value their
confidence. This evening we shall discuss
the details.

Blum. We thank you, Colonel. The
entire city will be pleased to learn of your
decision.

Col. Good-by till this evening. (*Exeunt the gentlemen. Col., alone, musingly.*)
I ought not to have accepted so quickly—
but I was obliged to do the Minister of
War the favor.—What will the girls say to
it? And Oldendorf?

(*Enter Oldendorf.*)

There he is now. (*Clears his throat.*)
He will be amazed! I cannot help him.
He must withdraw. Good day, Professor.
You come opportunely.

Old. (*Hastily.*) Colonel, it is rumored
in the city that Herr von Senden's party
has selected you as its candidate. I beg

you to assure me yourself that you would not accept such a nomination.

Col. If the offer was made to me, why should I not accept it as well as you? Yes, rather than you? For the motives that influence me are certainly sounder than your reasons.

Old. Then there is something in the rumor after all?

Col. Frankly, it is the truth. I have accepted. You see in me your opponent.

Old. That is the worst of all that has darkened our relations, so far. Colonel, could not the memory of a friendship which was hearty and undisturbed for years induce you to avoid this odious strife?

Col. I could not do otherwise, Oldendorf, believe me. It is now up to you to recall our old friendship. You are the younger man, to say nothing of other considerations, and it is now your place to step back.

Old. (*More excitedly.*) Colonel, I have known you for years. I know how active and warm your feelings are, and how little your fiery disposition is adapted to bear the petty vexations of every-day politics, the wearing struggle of debate. O, my worthy friend, listen to my entreaties, and take back your consent.

Col. Leave that to me. I am a tough old piece of timber. Think of yourself, my dear Oldendorf. You are young. You have a reputation as a scholar; your learning assures you of every sort of success. To what end do you wish to bring onto yourself nothing but hatred, ridicule and slights, instead of honor and recognition? For with your views that would not fail to come. Consider that. Be sensible and withdraw.

Old. Colonel, if I were able to follow my own wishes, I would do it on the spot. However, I am committed to my friends in this contest. I cannot draw back now.

Col. (*Excitedly.*) And I, also, cannot draw back, without injuring the cause. There we are—just as we were in the beginning. (*To himself.*) Stubborn! (*Each walks up and down on different sides of the stage.*) But you have no prospect at all of being elected, Oldendorf. It is certain that the majority of votes belongs to my friends. You expose yourself to an open defeat. (*Good-naturedly.*) I would not want you to be beaten before everybody by me. That would cause scandal and gossip. Do consider that! It is useless, entirely, for you to challenge to a duel.

Old. Even if all that were as certain as

you assume, Colonel, I would still be
obliged to hold out to the very end. But
as far as I can estimate the temper of the
people, the result is not so sure; and consider, Colonel, if it should happen that you
lost——

Col. (*Irritably.*) But I tell you it will
not happen!

Old. But if, as is possible, it did. How
disagreeable that would be for us both!
With what sensations would you look at
me then! I, perhaps, might welcome a defeat, but it would be a deep mortification
to you; and, Colonel, I fear this possi-
bility.

Col. Then for that very reason you
should withdraw.

Old. I cannot now, but you could yet.

Col. (*Heatedly.*) Confound it, sir, I
have said ''Yes.'' I am not the man to
follow it up with ''No.'' (*Both pace up
and down.*) Then this settles it, Professor.
My wishes are nothing to you. I might
have known that. Each of us goes his own
way. We have become public opponents.
We will be honorable enemies.

Old. (*Grasping   the   Col.'s   hand.*)
Colonel, I regard this day as a most unfortunate one, for I foresee sad consequences following it. Rest assured that,

under no circumstances will my love and loyalty to you be impaired.

Col. At last, our position is that before a battle. You wish to be beaten by an old soldier. You shall have your wish.

Old. I beg permission to inform Ida of our conversation.

Col. (*Somewhat disturbed.*) It is better that you do not do that now, Professor. An opportunity will be found. At present the ladies are dressing. I, myself, will tell them all that is necessary.

Old. Farewell, Colonel, and think of me without resentment.

Col. I will do the utmost, Professor. (*Exit Oldendorf.*) He has not yielded. What ambition possesses these scholars!

(*Enter Ida and Adelheid.*)

Ida. Was not that Oldendorf's voice?

Col. Yes, my child.

Adel. And he is gone again? Has anything happened?

Col. Assuredly, girls. Briefly, Oldendorf is not to be the deputy from this city, but I myself.

Adel.⎫ (*Together.*) ⎰You, Colonel?
Ida. ⎭   ⎱You, father?

Ida. Has Oldendorf withdrawn?

Adel. Is the election over?

Col. Neither one. Oldendorf has proven his much boasted attachment to us by not withdrawing, and election day is not yet over. Yet, according to all that I hear, there is no doubt that Oldendorf will be defeated.

Ida. And you, father, have become his opponent before all the world?

Adel. And what did Oldendorf say to that, Colonel?

Col. Don't get me excited, girls. Oldendorf was stubborn, but otherwise his behavior was quite correct, and as far as he is concerned everything is all right. The reasons which induced me to make the sacrifice are very important ones. I shall explain them to you another time. The matter is decided. I have accepted. Let that suffice for the present.

Ida. But, father, dear——

Col. Leave me in peace, Ida. I have to think of other things. This evening I am to speak in public. That is the established custom at such elections. Do not worry, my child. We will soon get the better of the Professor and his following. (*Exit Col. towards the garden. Ida and Adelheid stand opposite each other, wringing their hands.*)

Ida. What do you say to that?

Adel. You are his daughter. What do you say?

Ida. To think of it! My father!

Scarcely has he finished explaining to us thoroughly what cloaks of petty ambition surround these elections——

Adel. Yes, he did describe them right graphically—all the garments and mantles of vanity.

Ida. And the very next hour he has the mantle hung about himself! That is really preposterous! And what if my father is not elected? It was wrong of Oldendorf not to yield to my father's foibles. Is that your love for me, Herr Professor? Even he has not considered me!

Adel. I'll tell you what! We'll wish that they both fail! These politicians! It was hard enough for you when only one was pursuing politics; now that both are drinking of the soul-deluding beverage you are done for in any case. If I should ever reach the point of making a man my husband I would impose one condition on him—the wise precept of my old aunt: "Smoke tobacco, my husband, as much as you will. At the most it only spoils the carpets; but do not dare to ever look at a newspaper. That spoils your character."

(*Korb at the door.*)

What news, Korb?

Korb. (*Hurriedly, mysteriously.*) It is not true!

Adel. (*Ditto.*) What is not true?

Korb. That he is engaged to be married. He isn't thinking of that. His friends say he has only one beloved.

Adel. (*Excited.*) Who is that?

Korb. His newspaper.

Adel. (*Relieved.*) Oh! (*Aloud.*) One can see, then, how much untruth people speak. That will do, my dear Korb. (*Exit Korb.*)

Ida. What is untrue?

Adel. Oh, that we women are cleverer than the men! We talk just as wisely, and I fear we are just as prone to forget our wisdom at the first opportunity. We are all of us poor sinners.

Ida. You can jest. You have never experienced having your father and beloved friend arrayed against each other.

Adel. Do you think so? I did have, however, a good little friend who had very foolishly bestowed her heart on a handsome, spirited young fellow. She was still a child at the time and it was a very touching relation. Knightly homage on his part, and tender sighs on hers. Then the young heroine had the misfortune to become jealous and she so far forgot poetry and propriety as to slap her heart's chosen cavalier. It was only a very gentle slap, but it became a fateful one. The young lady's father had seen it and required an explanation. Then the young knight did what a true hero must ever do. He assumed the entire blame, and told the irate father that he had demanded a kiss of the lady—the poor youth! Such presumption he never had!—a blow had been the answer. The father was a stern man. He handled the young man severely. The hero was banished from his family, from his home, and the heroine sat, solitary, in her tower, and wept for the lost one.

Ida. She should have told her father the truth.

Adel. Oh, she did, but her confession only made the trouble worse. Many years have passed since that time, and the knight and his lady are now old people and very sensible.

Ida. (*Smiling.*) And don't they love each other any more, since they are sensible?

Adel. Dear child, I cannot say positively how the gentleman feels. He wrote a very beautiful letter to the young lady after the death of her father. Further than that I know nothing; but the lady has more confidence than you. She is still hoping all the time. (*Seriously.*) Yes, she is hoping and her father himself allowed it before his death—you see she is still hoping.

Ida. (*Embracing her.*) And who is the injured person in whom she is hoping?

Adel. Be still, my darling. That is a dark secret. Very few living men know about that; and when the birds in the trees at Rosenau tell each other of it, they deal with the story as an obscure legend of their forefathers. They sing softly and plaintively, and their feathers bristle with awe. In due time you shall find it all out. For the present think of the club reception and how beautiful you are going to look.

Ida. On one side my father, on the other my lover—how is it to end?

Adel. Never mind. The one is an old soldier, the other a young statesman. In all ages that sort of public characters has always been wound around the little fingers of us women. (*Exeunt both.*)

SECOND SCENE

(Side rooms off from an open hall. In the rear a row of columns and pillars, between which one looks into the illuminated hall, and behind that into another. Forward, left, a door. Right, tables and chairs; chandeliers; later, from time to time, music in the distance.

In the hall, gentlemen and ladies are standing or walking up and down in groups.)

(Enter Senden, Blumenberg; behind them,
        Schmock, out of the hall.)

Send. Everything goes well. There is a fine spirit among the company. These good burghers are charmed over our arrangement. That idea of yours, of having a reception, was a first-rate one, Blumenberg.

Blum. Hurry up then and get some life into the people. A little music would do good service to begin with; the Viennese waltzes are best on account of the women. Then comes a speech by yourself, then several songs, and at supper the introduction of the Colonel and the toasts. It cannot fail! The people must have hearts of stone if they do not give their votes in gratitude for such a reception.

Send. The toasts are assigned.

Blum. But the music! Why is the music silent?

Send. I am waiting till the arrival of the Colonel.

Blum. He must be received with a flourish of trumpets. That will flatter him, you know.

Send. It is ordered that way. A march

will begin immediately and we will lead
him in, in procession.

Blum. Splendid! That will add solem-
nity to his entrance. Think of your speech,
though. Make it of popular tone, for to-
day we are with the masses.

(*Enter guests, among them Henning.*)

Send. (*Doing the honors with Blumenberg.*) Very glad to see you here. We
knew that you wouldn't fail us. Is this
your lady?

Guest. Yes, this is my wife, Herr von
Senden.

Send. You with us too, Herr Henning?
Welcome, good sir.

Henn. I was invited through my
friend, and furthermore, I was curious. I
hope my presence will not be disagreeable
to any one.

Send. Quite to the contrary. We are
delighted to greet you here. (*Exeunt
guests through centre door. Senden, in
conversation with them, exits also.*)

Blum. He knows how to manage the
people. That's what the good manners of
these gentlemen can accomplish. He is
useful. He is also useful to me. He manages the others and I manage him. (*Turning around, he notices Schmock, who is
loitering by the door.*) What are you doing here? Why do stand listening? You

aren't a toll-gate keeper. See to it that
you don't stay in my vicinity. Circulate
around among the company.

Schmock. Whom am I to go to when I
don't know a single person among the people? You are my only acquaintance here.

Blum. Why do you need to tell people
that I am your acquaintance? It is no
honor to stand beside you.

Schmock. Even if it is no honor, at
least it is no disgrace. I can go alone also.

Blum. Have you money so that you can
get something to eat? Go to the proprietor
of the restaurant and have him give you
something in my name. The committee
will pay for it.

Schmock. I won't go away to eat. I
don't need to spend anything. I have
eaten. (*Distant flourish and march. Exit
Blumenberg. Schmock alone. Coming forward. Furiously.*) I hate him! I shall
tell him that I hate him and despise him
from the bottom of my heart. (*Turns to
go. Returning.*) I cannot tell him yet, for
then he will reject all the copy that I
make for the paper. I'll see whether I can
swallow it. (*Exit centre door.*)

(*Enter Bolz, Kämpe, Bellmaus outside
door.*)

Bolz. (*Marching in.*) Here we are in
the house of Capulet. (*Pantomime of

sheathing swords.) Conceal thy swords
'neath roses, puff out thy cheeks, and seem
as dull and innocent as possible.   Above
all, start not any quarrels, I beg of you,
and if thou meet'st this Tybalt, Senden,
then be good and slip away around that
nook.   (*Through the rear halls a polonaise
is seen going on.*)   You, Romeo Bellmaus,
beware of the females!   In there I see
more curls flying and handkerchiefs wav-
ing than are good for your peace of mind.

Kämpe. Wager me a bottle of cham-
pagne that if one of us gets into quarrels,
you will be the one.

Bolz. Possibly; but I promise you that
you will surely have your share.   Now
listen to my plan of campaign.   You,
Kämpe——

(*Enter Schmock.*)

Hold!   Who is there?   Confound it!
The *Coriolanus'* office boy!   Our incognito
has not lasted long.

Schmock. (*Who, before the last words,
was visible, standing observantly at the
door, advancing.*)   I wish you a pleasant
evening, Herr Bolz.

Bolz. I wish you the same, of still pleas-
anter quality, Herr Schmock.

Schmock. Could I speak a few words
with you?

Bolz. A few? Do not ask too few, noble

armor-bearer of the *Coriolanus*. Two dozen words you shall have, but not more.

Schmock. Couldn't you give me employment on your paper?

Bolz. (*To Kämpe and Bellmaus.*) Do you hear? On our paper? Hm! You demand much, noble Roman!

Schmock. I am sick of the *Coriolanus*. I should be willing to do everything for you that you have to do. I should like to be with honorable men, where one gets his due, and fair treatment.

Bolz. What do you want of us, slave of Rome? That we should withdraw you from your party? Never! That we should do violence to your political convictions? Make you an apostate? That we should bear the guilt of your coming into our party? Never! Our conscience is tender. It rebels against your proposition.

Schmock. Why should you worry about that? I have learned from Blumenberg how to write on all sides. I have written on the Liberal side and again on the Conservative side. I can write on any side.

Bolz. I see that you have character. You are sure of success on our paper. Your offer honors us, but we cannot accept it now. Such a world-affecting occurrence, as your conversion, calls for mature consideration. Meanwhile you will

not have given your confidence to an un-
feeling barbarian. (*Aside to the others.*)
Perhaps there is something to be gotten
out of him. Bellmaus, you have the best
heart among us three. You must take him
in hand to-day.

Bellmaus. But what am I to do with
him?

Bolz. Lead him to the restaurant. Sit
down with him in a corner, and pour punch
into every cranny of his poor head till his
secrets spring out like wet mice. Make him
chatter, especially over the election. Go
along, little one, but be very prudent lest
you grow excited yourself and talk too
much.

Bell. At this rate I shall not see much
of the reception.

Bolz. That you won't, son! But what
does the reception amount to for you?
Heat, dust and old dance music! Besides,
we'll tell you everything to-morrow, and
anyway, you are a poet and can imagine
the whole thing much more beautifully
than it really is. Do not grieve on that
account. Your rôle seems thankless, but it
is the most important of all, for it re-
quires coolness and craftiness. Go, my
mouse, and take care not to get warmed
up yourself.

Bell. I'll take care, Herr Cat. Come,

Schmock! (*Exeunt Bellmaus and Schmock.*)

Bolz. It will be well if we separate, also.

Kämpe. I go to draw out opinions. If I need you I'll hunt you up.

Bolz. I dare not show myself much. I'll remain here in the vicinity. (*Exit Kämpe.*) Alone at last! (*Goes to centre door.*) There stands the Colonel, surrounded by a dense circle. It is she! She is here and I must lie in hiding, like a fox among leaves! But she has falcon eyes— perhaps—the group is breaking up—she is going arm in arm with Ida through the hall. (*Animatedly.*) They are coming nearer! (*Angrily.*) Oh, woe! There is Korb rushing up to me! Now, of all times! (*Enter Korb.*)

Korb. Herr Konrad, I do not trust my eyes! You here at this reception?

Bolz. Be still, old man. I am not here without reason. I can rely on you. You belong to us.

Korb. Body and soul. In all this speechifying and fiddling I cry out secretly, "Long live the *Union!*" Here it is. (*Shows a paper in his pocket.*)

Bolz. Good, Korb. You can do me a favor. In a corner of the restaurant sits Bellmaus beside a stranger. He is to extract information from the stranger, but he cannot carry much himself, and is made garrulous easily. You will do the party a great service if you will hurry down there and drink punch in order to support Bell-maus. That *you* can stand it, I know of old.

Korb. (*Quickly.*) I go. You always have tricks in your head. Leave it to me. The stranger shall lose, and the *Union* shall triumph. (*Exits hurriedly. The music ceases.*)

Bolz. Poor Schmock! (*At the door.*) Ah! They are still going through the hall —Ida is accosted—she is standing still— Adelheid goes on—(*Excited.*)—she is com-ing—she is coming alone!

(*Enter Adelheid.*)

Adel. (*Passing the door, steps in quickly. Bolz bows.*) Konrad! Dear Doctor! (*Extends her hand.*)

Bolz. (*Bows deeply over her hand.*)

Adel. (*In joyful agitation.*) I recog-nized you immediately in the distance. Show me your face! Yes, it has changed but little. A scar—somewhat browner— and a little wrinkle around the mouth. I hope it comes from laughing.

Bolz. If, just now, anything is closer to me than laughing it is only a fleeting in-iquity of my soul. I see myself in dupli-cate, like a morose Highlander. With you my long happy childhood passes bodily before my eyes; everything that it brought of joy and pain I feel again as acutely as if I were still the boy who once marched into the forest for you, in search of adventure, and caught robins. And yet the beautiful form which I see before me is so different from that of my playmate, that I believe it is only a lovely dream I am dreaming. Your eyes shine as kindly as formerly, but—(*bowing slightly*)—I scarcely have the right to think of old dreams any more.

Adel. But perhaps I have not altered as much as you think. And however much we both may have changed, we have remained good friends, haven't we, Doctor?

Bolz. Rather than give up the smallest part of the right which I have to your interest I will write malicious articles against myself and print them and distribute them.

Adel. And yet you have become so haughty that you have not even sought for your friend in the city until to-day. Why are you a stranger to the Colonel's house?

Bolz. I am not unknown to it. On the contrary, I have a very enviable position there which I maintain best by going there as little as possible. The Colonel and sometimes even Fräulein Ida like to appease their anger against Oldendorf and the paper by seeing in me the evil one with hoofs and horns. Such a delicate relation must be handled with care. A devil cannot make himself so common as to appear every day.

Adel. But I beg you to give up this exalted position now. I shall remain in the city through the winter and I hope you will present yourself at the home of my friends, as a citizen of this world, for the sake of the comrade of your youth.

Bolz. In any rôle which you assign to me.

Adel. Even in that of a messenger of peace between the Colonel and Oldendorf?

Bolz. If peace is to be purchased only by Oldendorf's resignation, no. Otherwise I am ready for all good works.

Adel. And I fear that peace is to be purchased at that price alone. You see, Herr Konrad, even we have become opponents.

Bolz. To do anything against your will is monstrous to me, however much I may be a son of perdition. Then my saint wishes and demands that Oldendorf be not the representative?

Adel. I do wish and demand it, Sir Diabolus.

Bolz. It is hard. You have so many

gentlemen in your heaven to whom you can present Fräulein Ida. Why must you deprive a poor devil of his single soul, the Professor?

Adel. It is the Professor alone that I want and you are to surrender him to me.

Bolz. I am in despair. I would tear my hair if our location were not so unfavorable. I fear your displeasure. I tremble at the thought that this election may be distasteful to you.

Adel. Then try to prevent the election.

Bolz. That I cannot do, but as soon as it is past, my fate will be to mourn over your anger and to grow melancholy. I shall withdraw from the world, far away to the North Pole. There I shall sadly play dominoes with polar bears the rest of my days and promulgate the elements of journalistic education among the seals. That will be easier to bear than a wrathful glance from your eyes.

Adel. (*Laughing.*) You were always so. You used to promise everything possible and then were continually acting as you pleased. But before you go to the North Pole just try once more to appease me here. (*Kämpe appears at the door.*) Hush, now. I shall expect a call from you. Farewell, my refound friend! (*Exit.*)

Bolz. There, my good angel indignantly

turns her back on me! Now I have irre-
trievably fallen into your clutches, oh
witch Politics! (*Exits quickly, centre.*)
(*Enter Piepenbrink, Frau Piepenbrink,
    Bertha, escorted by Fritz Kleinmichel,
    and Kleinmichel through centre door.
    Quadrille behind the scenes.*)
Piep. Thank heaven, we have gotten
out of that crowd!

Frau Piep. It is very hot!

Klein. And the music is too loud.
There are too many trumpets in it and
trumpets are always disagreeable to me.

Piep. Here is a quiet spot. We'll sit
down here.

Fritz. Bertha would like to stay in the
hall longer. Couldn't I go back with her?

Piep. I have nothing against you people going back to the hall, but I prefer
that you stay with us. I like to have all my
folks together.

Frau Piep. Stay with your parents, my
child.

Piep. Sit down. (*To his wife.*) You
sit down in the corner. Fritz comes next
to me. Take Bertha between you, neighbors. She will come to your table soon,
anyway.

Fritz. When will that "soon" be, godfather? You have been saying that for a

long time and then putting the wedding off farther and farther.

Piep. That is none of your business.

Fritz. Why, godfather, I thought that I was surely the one that Bertha is to marry.

Piep. That is a fine thing! Any one might wish that! But I am the one who is to give her to you, youngster, and that means more, for I find it hard enough to let my little wagtail out of the nest. Therefore wait! You shall have her, but wait.

Klein. He will wait, neighbor.

Piep. I should most assuredly advise him to. Hey! Waiter! Waiter!

Frau Piep. How poor the service is in such places!

Piep. Waiter! (*Waiter comes.*) My name is Piepenbrink. I have brought with me six bottles of my own wine. You are assistant to the proprietor. I want them brought here. (*While the waiter is fetching bottles and glasses, Bolz and Kämpe come forward by the door. Waiter back and forth in the rear.*)

Bolz. (*Aside to Kämpe.*) Which one is it?

Kämpe. The one with his back turned to us, the one with the broad shoulders.

Bolz. And what sort of business does he have?

Kämpe. Mostly red wine.

Bolz. Good! (*Aloud.*) Waiter, a table and two chairs! A bottle of red wine! (*Waiter brings the things ordered to the foreground, left.*)

Frau Piep. What do they want here?

Piep. The unpleasant part of such mixed gatherings is that one cannot be alone anywhere.

Klein. They seem to be respectable men. I believe that I have seen one of them before.

Piep. (*Decidedly.*) Respectable or not, they are inconvenient for us.

Klein. To be sure they are.

Bolz. (*Seating himself with Kämpe.*) Well, I suppose we can sit here in peace over a bottle of red wine, my friend. I scarcely have the courage to pour it, for the wine in such restaurants is always frightful. What sort of stuff is this, I wonder?

Piep. (*Provoked.*) So? Just listen!

Kämpe. Let's try it. (*Pours, then says softly.*) There is a P.P. on the seal. That might mean Piepenbrink.

Piep. I really am curious to see what these upstarts will take exception to in the wine.

Frau Piep. Hush, Philipp. They will hear you!

Bolz. (*Softly.*) You surely were right.

The proprietor gets his wine from him for
that reason he comes here.

Piep. They don't seem to be thirsty at
all. They aren't drinking.

Bolz. (*Tastes. Aloud.*) Not bad!

Piep. (*Ironically.*) So?

Bolz. (*Tastes again.*) A good, pure
wine!

Piep. (*Recovering.*) The man hasn't
bad judgment.

Bolz. But, after all, it doesn't compare
with a similar wine which I drank recently
at a friend's home.

Piep. So?

Bolz. Since that time, I know that there
is only one man in the city of whom a
discriminating wine drinker may get his
red wine.

Kämpe. And he is?

Piep. (*Ironically.*) I *am* curious.

Bolz. A certain Piepenbrink.

Piep. (*Pleased, nodding his head.*)
Good!

Kämpe. Yes, the business has an excellent reputation, everywhere.

Piep. They do not know that their wine
is also out of my cellars. Ha, ha, ha!

Bolz. (*Turning to him.*) Are you
laughing at us, sir?

Piep. Ha, ha, ha! Nothing bad. I
only heard you discussing the wine. So

Piepenbrink's wine tastes better to you than this? Ha, ha, ha!

Bolz. (*With mild anger.*) Sir, I must entreat you to find my expression less comic. I do not know Herr Piepenbrink, but I have the pleasure of knowing his wine, and therefore I repeat the statement that Piepenbrink has better wine in his cellar than this is here. Why do you find that laughable? You do not know Piepenbrink's wines and have no right at all to judge.

Piep. I do not know Piepenbrink's wines? I do not even know Philipp Piepenbrink? I have never seen his wife—d'ye hear that, Lotte? And if his daughter, Bertha, meets me, I say: "Who is this little black head?" That is a merry tale, isn't it, Kleinmichel? (*Laughs.*)

Klein. It is very laughable. (*Laughs.*)

Bolz. (*Standing up with dignity.*) Sir, I am a stranger to you, and have never injured you. You have a respectable appearance and I find you in the company of admirable ladies. For that reason I cannot believe that you have come here to ridicule strangers. So, as a man, I ask you for an explanation of why you find my innocent words so remarkable. If you are an enemy of Herr Piepenbrink, why do you make us suffer for that?

Piep. (*Rising.*) Now, don't get excited, sir. Just listen! The wine which you are drinking here is also out of Piepenbrink's cellar and I myself am Philipp Piepenbrink, for whose sake you are pitching into me. Now, you understand why I laugh?

Bolz. Ah! Stands the matter so? You are Herr Piepenbrink himself? I am sincerely pleased to make your acquaintance. No offense meant, honored sir.

Piep. No, no offense meant. It is all right.

Bolz. Since you were so kind as to give us your name, then it is also in order that you learn ours. Doctor of Philosophy Bolz, and here my friend, Herr Kämpe.

Piep. Delighted.

Bolz. We are somewhat strange in the company and withdrew into this side room, for one is not exactly at ease among so many unfamiliar faces. We should be very sorry, however, to mar, in the least, by our presence the pleasure of the ladies and the conversation of so estimable a company. Tell us frankly if we inconvenience you and we will seek another place.

Piep. You seem to be a jolly fellow and do not inconvenience me by any means. Dr. Bolz—that was the name, wasn't it?

Frau Piep. We are not acquainted here

either and have just now sat down. Piepenbrink! (*Nudges him gently.*)

Piep. I'll tell you what, Dr. Bolz—
since you already know the yellow seal out
of my cellar and have shown wise judgment, as it were, would you try it here
once more? This brand will taste better
to you. Sit down by us, if you have nothing better to do and we will chat a bit
together.

Bolz. (*With composure, as in the whole
scene, throughout which he, as well as
Kämpe, must not appear officious.*) That is
a very friendly invitation and we accept it
with thanks. Have the goodness, most excellent sir, to make us acquainted with
your party.

Piep. This one, here, is my wife.

Bolz. Do not be displeased over our intrusion, madame. We promise to be right
well behaved and as good company as is
possible for two shy young fellows.

Piep. Here is my daughter.

Bolz. (*To Frau Piepenbrink.*) That
was to be inferred from the resemblance.

Piep. Here is Herr Kleinmichel, my
friend, and here, Fritz Kleinmichel, my
daughter's intended.

Bolz. I congratulate you, gentlemen, on
such charming neighbors. (*To Piepenbrink.*) Permit me to sit beside the lady

of the house. Kämpe, I should think you might take the seat by Herr Kleinmichel. (*They sit down.*) Now we are arranged, alternately. Waiter! (*Waiter steps up to him.*) Two bottles of this wine, here.

Piep. Wait a minute! You will not find this wine here. I brought my own with me. You must drink with me.

Bolz. But, Herr Piepenbrink——

Piep. Not a word! You are to drink with me—and when I say to any one that he is to drink with me, sir, I do not mean sip, like women, but drain and fill up your glass again. Govern yourself accordingly.

Bolz. Good! I am content. We accept your hospitality as gratefully as you have offered it cordially; but you must permit me, then, to reciprocate. Next Sunday you will all be my guests, won't you? Say "Yes," my kind host! Punctually at seven o'clock a sociable supper. I am unmarried, so in a respectable hotel. Give your consent, honored lady—your hand on it, Herr Piepenbrink. Yours, also, Herr Kleinmichel and Herr Fritz. (*Holds out his hand to all of them.*)

Piep. If my wife is satisfied, I certainly would like to do so.

Bolz. Accepted. Settled. And now the first toast! The good spirit who has brought us together to-day—long may he

live—(*inquiringly*)—what is the **name of**
that spirit?

Fritz. Chance.

Bolz. No, he wears a yellow cap.

Piep. He is called the "Yellow Seal."

Bolz. Correct. Here's to his health!
We wish the gentleman a right long life,
as the cat said to the bird when she bit his
head off.

Klein. We wish him a long life while
making it short.

Bolz. Well said! Vivat!

Piep. Vivat! (*They clink glasses.
Piep. to his wife.*) We'll have a good time
yet to-day.

Frau Piep. They are very genteel, nice
people.

Bolz. You cannot imagine how happy I
am that our good fortune led us into such
excellent company. It is true that everything in there is beautifully arranged——

Piep. It can't be denied that the ar-
rangements are very satisfactory.

Bolz. Very satisfactory! But this political gathering is not to my taste.

Piep. Indeed? You probably don't belong to the party and so it does not please
you.

Bolz. That isn't it. But when I consider that they are not invited together so
that they may be heartily entertained, but

so that they may give their vote to this or that man, then I lose my enthusiasm.

Piep. But that won't be so. We should have something to say about that, eh, old fellow?

Klein. I hope that it will imply no obligations.

Bolz. Perhaps not. I have no vote to give away, and I say, give me a gathering where one thinks of nothing else but to enjoy his neighbor and to be attentive to the queens of the company, to the lovely women. Raise your glasses, gentleman, to the health of the ladies! The health of both who grace our circle!

Piep. Come here, Lotte. We want to drink your health.

Bolz. Fräulein, allow a stranger to drink to the happiness of your future.

Piep. What else is going on in there, I wonder.

Fritz. I hear that they are to have speeches at supper, and the candidate, Colonel Berg, is to be presented.

Piep. A very estimable gentleman.

Klein. Yes, it is a good choice which the gentlemen of the committee have made.

(*Enter Adelheid.*)

Adel. (*In background, then entering indifferently.*) Here he sits! What sort of a company is that?

Kämpe. They say that Professor Oldendorf has great prospect of being elected. There should be a good many who will vote for him.

Piep. I have nothing against him, but he is too young for my liking.

(*Enter Senden—later Blumenberg and guests.*)

Senden. (*In background.*) You here, Fräulein?

Adel. I am amusing myself by watching these queer people. They act as if they were the sole remaining people on the earth.

Send. What do I see? There sits the *Union* itself, and with one of the most important persons at the reception. (*Music ceases.*)

Bolz. (*Who meanwhile is conversing with Frau Piepenbrink, but has listened attentively—to Frau Piepenbrink.*) Ah, you see, the gentlemen could not keep from talking politics. Did you not mention Professor Oldendorf?

Piep. Yes, my merry Doctor, very casually.

Bolz. If you are talking of him, I earnestly beg you to speak only good of him, for he is the best and noblest man that I know.

Piep. So? You know him?

Klein. You are one of his friends, then?

Bolz. More than that. If the Professor should say to me to-day, "Bolz, it is advantageous to me that you jump into the water," jump in I would, disagreeable as it would be just now for me to be drowned in water.

Piep. Oho, that is putting it pretty strong!

Bolz. I have no right to take part in a discussion of candidates in this company, but if I should have a deputy to choose it would necessarily be he first of all.

Piep. You are much taken with the man then?

Bolz. His political views do not concern me much; but what do I require in a representative? That he be a man; that he have a warm heart and a safe judgment, and know beyond doubt or question what is good and right; and then that he have the strength to do what he recognizes to be right, without wavering, without hesitancy.

Piep. Bravo!

Klein. But the Colonel is such a man also.

Bolz. Possibly he is—I do not know; but I do know about Oldendorf. I have looked deep into his heart during an accident that happened to me. I was once about to be burned to powder, when he had the coolness to prevent it. I am indebted to him that I sit here. He saved my life.

Send. He lies frightfully. (*Starts forward.*)

Adel. (*Holding him back.*)   Be still! I believe there is some truth in the story.

Piep. Now, his saving your life was fine. At the same time, similar things occur often.

Frau Piep. Tell us about it, anyway, Doctor.

Bolz. The little incident is like hundreds of others, and it would be of no special interest to me had it not been my own experience. Imagine an old house. I am a student and lodge there, on the fourth floor. In the house opposite me a young scholar is rooming. We do not know each other. In the middle of the night a fearful noise and a remarkable crackling below awaken me. If it was mice, they certainly were executing a torch dance, for my room was brilliantly lighted. I spring to the window; there the bright flames shoot way up to me from the story beneath; my window panes are cracking around my head and vile smoke bursts upon me. Since it becomes uncomfortable, under these circumstances, to lean out of the window, I run to the door and

open it. Even the stairs cannot escape the
common fate of old wood. They are burn-
ing brightly. On the fourth floor up, and
no way of escape! I give myself up for
lost! Half unconscious, I rushed back to
the window. ·I heard some one down on
the street shout, "A man, a man! Bring a
ladder!" A ladder was placed. It in-
stantly began to smoke and burn like tinder.
It was snatched away. Then streams of
water from all the fire engines fell hissing
on the flames under me. I heard plainly
when every single stream struck the glow-
ing wall. A new ladder was placed. It
was deathly still below, and you can well
imagine that I didn't have any desire to
make a commotion in my fiery oven, either.
Below the people were calling, "It won't
reach!" and then a deep voice rang out,
"Higher with the ladder!" You see, I
knew on the spot that this was the voice
of my rescuer. "Quick!" called the people below. Then a fresh cloud of steam
forced its way into the room. I had swal-
lowed enough of the thick smoke and I fell
down on the floor by the window.

Frau Piep. Poor Doctor!

Piep. (*Excitedly.*) Go on!

Send. (*Starts to hurry forward.*)

Adel. (*Restraining him.*) Please let
him finish. The story is true.

Bolz. Then a man's hand grasped me by the back of the neck, a rope was slung under my arms and a mighty hand raised me from the floor. A moment later I was upon the ladder, half carried, half dragged. I reached the pavement, unconscious and with shirt on fire. I came to in the chamber of the young scholar. Except for several small burns I had brought nothing over to my new lodging. All my possessions were burned. The stranger nursed me and cared for me like one brother for the other. Not until I was able to be out again did I learn that this scholar, who had taken me in with him, was the same man who had visited me that night on the ladder. You see, the man's heart is in the right place, and therefore I want him to become the deputy, and therefore I could do for him what I would not do for myself. I could electioneer for him, scheme for him, and make fools out of honest people for him. This man is Professor Oldendorf.

Piep. He is surely an out and out honorable man. (*Rising.*) Long life to him! Up! (*All stand and clink glasses.*)

Bolz. (*Bowing to them all. To Frau Piepenbrink.*) I see ardent sympathy shining in your eyes, noble lady, and I thank you for it. Herr Piepenbrink, I beg permission to shake your hand. You are a splendid man. (*Slaps him on the back, embraces him.*) Give me your hand, Herr Kleinmichel! (*Embraces him.*) You also, Herr Fritz Kleinmichel! May no child of yours ever be in a fire, but if he is may there always be a brave man at hand to bring him out. Come nearer. I must embrace you also.

Frau Piep. (*With emotion.*) Piepenbrink, we are having roast veal to-morrow. What do you think? (*Talks with him softly.*)

Adel. He is becoming irrepressible!

Send. He is insufferable! I see that you are indignant as well as myself. He is getting the people away from us. It is not to be endured longer.

Bolz. (*Who had gone around the table, turning back, standing still before Frau Piepenbrink.*) It is really too bad to stop here. Herr Piepenbrink, head of the house, I beg for permission—the hand or the mouth?

Adel. (*Anxiously coming forward on the right side.*) He is really going to kiss her!

Piep. Go ahead, old fellow! Courage!

Frau Piep. Piepenbrink, I am surprised at you!

Adel. (*At the instant when Bolz is about to kiss Frau Piepenbrink, goes past *him, as if accidentally, across the stage, and holds her bouquet between Bolz and Frau Piepenbrink. Softly and hastily to Bolz.)* You go too far! You are observed! *(Goes from left to rear and exits.)*

Bolz. A fairy intervenes!

Send. (Who has already, before this, been speaking to several other guests, among them Blumenberg, at the same moment advances noisily. To the party at the table.) He is presuming, he has intruded!

Piep. (Striking the table and rising.) Oho, that's a pretty howdy-do, I must say! If I kiss my wife, or let her be kissed, it is nobody's business! Nobody's! Not a man, not a woman, not a fairy has the right to lay hand before her mouth!

Bolz. Quite right! Splendid! Hear! Hear!

Send. My dear Herr Piepenbrink! Nothing against you! The company is delighted to see you in this place. It is only Herr Bolz, whose presence here, we notice, is causing a sensation. He holds such entirely different political views that we are forced to regard his appearance at this reception as an unwarrantable intrusion.

Bolz. I hold different political views? I recognize, in company, no other political principle than to drink with honest people and not to drink with those whom I do not consider honest. With you, sir, I have not drunk.

Piep. (*Striking the table.*) A good shot!

Send. (*Hotly.*) You have forced your way in here!

Bolz. (*Indignantly.*) Forced?

Piep. Forced? Old boy, you surely have an entrance card?

Bolz. (*With an air of virtue.*) Here is my card! I do not show it to you, but to this gentleman, with whom you wish to bring me into disrepute by this attack. Kämpe, give your card to Herr Piepenbrink! He is the one to judge on all the cards in the world.

Piep. Here are two cards which are just as correct as mine. You have distributed them in all directions, like sour grapejuice. Ho! ho! I see plainly how the matter stands. I do not belong to your set either, but you want me to; therefore you have been running into my house two or three times because you thought to catch me. Since I am a voter, I am of importance to you; but this gentleman is not a voter; he is of no importance to you. We are on to such tricks!

Send. But, Herr Piepenbrink——

Piep. (*Interrupting him more vehemently.*) Is it right to insult a peaceable

guest on that account? Is it right to stop
my wife's lips? That is an injustice to this
man! He is to remain here, now, and
whoever ventures to attack him has me to
deal with!

Bolz. Your hand, good sir! You are a
true comrade. So hand in hand with thee,
I defy the Capulet and his whole tribe!

Piep. With *thee!* You are right, old
boy! Come here! They can rage till they
burst! To good fellowship! (*They drink
brotherhood.*)

Bolz. Long live Piepenbrink!

Piep. So, old man! And I'll tell you
something. Since we are so contented together, I suggest that we let these people
here do what they please, and all of you
come to my house. There I will brew a
bowl of punch and we will have a good
time together, jolly as pipers. I will escort
you. You others go on ahead!

Send. (*And guests.*) But just listen,
dear Herr Piepenbrink!

Piep. I will hear nothing, not another
word!

(*Enter Bellmaus; still more guests.*)

Bell. (*Coming hurriedly through the
crowd.*) Here I am!

Bolz. My nephew! Gracious, madame,
I place him under your protection.
Nephew, you take Madame Piepenbrink.

(*Frau Piep. grasps Bellmaus firmly by the arm and holds him fast. Polka behind the scenes.*) Farewell, gentlemen. You are not in a position to spoil our good humor. There, the music is beginning. We will march in festive array, and once more I will shout in conclusion, "Long live Piepenbrink!" (*Those who are departing say, "Long live Piepenbrink!" They march out in triumph. Fritz Kleinmichel with his fiancée, Kämpe with Kleinmichel, Frau Piepenbrink with Bellmaus, last of all Bolz with Piepenbrink.*)

(*Enter the Colonel.*)

Col. What is going on in here?

Send. A contemptible scandal! The *Union* has enticed both of our most important voters away from us! (*Curtain falls.*)

THIRD ACT

SCENE: *Summer parlor in the Colonel's house*

(Colonel in the foreground, pacing up and down with heavy steps. In the rear, Adelheid and Ida, arm in arm, the latter in great agitation. Short pause; then enter Senden.)

Send. (*Calling hurriedly through the centre door.*) It is going well! Thirty-seven votes against twenty-nine!

Col. Who has thirty-seven votes?

Send. Naturally, you, Colonel.

Col. Naturally. (*Exit Senden.*) Election day is unbearable! In no affair of my life have I ever had this feeling of anxiety! It is a miserable fear, which is not becoming for even a color sergeant. (*Stamping foot.*) Damn! (*Goes towards rear.*)

Ida. (*Stepping forward with Adelheid.*) This uncertainty is terrible! I only know one thing. I shall be unhappy, however the election turns out. (*Leans on Adelheid.*)

Adel. Courage! Courage, my little girl! Everything may be all right. Con-

96

ceal your anxiety from your father. He is in a frame of mind that does not please me, without that.

(*Enter Blumenberg hastily by the door, Colonel opposite him.*)

Col. Now, sir, how does it stand?

Blum. Forty-one votes for you, Colonel, thirty-four for our opponent; three votes have fallen to others. The votes are coming in at long intervals now, but the difference in your favor remains pretty much the same. Eight more votes for you, Colonel, and the victory is won. There is now the greatest probability that we win. I am hurrying back for the crisis is approaching. I take my leave of the ladies! (*Exits.*)

Col. Ida!

Ida. (*Hurries up to him.*)

Col. Are you my good daughter?

Ida. My dear father!

Col. I know what is worrying you, my child. You suffer the most in this. Be of good cheer, Ida. If, as now appears, the young knight of the quill has to yield the palm to the old soldier, we will talk further, then. Oldendorf has not deserved that much from me. There is a great deal about him that vexes me; but you are my only child. I shall think of that alone. The point now is to break down the youth's defiance. (*Releases Ida, walks up and down again.*)

Adel. (*In the foreground, to herself.*)
The barometer is rising, the sun of favor is
breaking through the clouds! If only
everything were over! Such excitement is
contagious! (*To Ida.*) You see, it isn't
necessary yet for you to enter a convent.

Ida. But if Oldendorf is defeated, how
will he bear it?

Adel. (*Shrugging her shoulders.*) He
will lose a seat in uncomfortable society
and gain in its stead an amusing little
wife. I should think he might be satisfied.
In any case he will have an opportunity
of making his speeches. What does it matter whether he makes them in this or that
Chamber? I believe you will listen to him
more reverently than any deputy.

Ida. (*Timidly.*) But, Adelheid, sup-
posing it were better for the country that
Oldendorf should be elected?

Adel. Well, my treasure, then there is
no help for the country. Our state, and
the other countries in Europe, will have to
devise some means of getting along without
the Professor. You yourself are to be considered first. You will marry him. You
have the preference.

(*Enter Karl.*)

Adel. What news, Karl?

Karl. Herr von Senden presents his compliments to you, and announces: forty-seven to forty-two. The commissioner of the election has already congratulated him.

Col. Congratulated? Have my uniform in order, get the key to the wine cellar and have things in readiness, for it is possible we may have visitors this evening.

Karl. As you direct, Colonel. (*Exits.*)

Col. (*To himself, in foreground.*) Now, my young Professor! My style does not please you! It may be— I grant that you are a better journalist. Here, however, in practical matters, for once you shall not have your own way. (*Pause.*) Perhaps it will be necessary for me to say a few words to-night. In my regiment I had the reputation of always knowing how to speak to the point, but in these civilian maneuvers I feel a little uncertainty. Let us consider! It will be fitting that I mention Oldendorf in my speech, with respect and approval, of course. Yes, indeed, I must do that. He is an upright man, with an excellent heart, and a scholar of good judgment, and he can be very genial, if one disregards his political theories. We have spent many happy evenings with each other and whenever we sat together around my fat tea-kettle and the honest youth began to tell his stories, Ida's eyes would be

fixed on his face and would shine with de-
light, and I believe my old eyes would, too.
Those were splendid evenings. Why don't
we have them any more? Bah! They will
come back. He will bear his defeat in
silence, as is his way—a good, comfortable
way! No touchiness about him! At heart
he is an excellent man and Ida and I would
be very happy with him. And, therefore,
gentlemen and voters— But, hang it all!
I can't say all that to the voters yet. I
shall say——

(*Enter Senden.*)

Send. (*Entering excitedly.*) Shameful! Shameful! All is lost!

Col. Ha! (*Assumes an attitude of military self-possession.*)

Ida. My presentiment! My
father! (*Hastens to him.*) }(*Together.*)
Adel. Oh, woe!

Send. The situation was first-rate. We
had forty-seven, the opponents forty-two
votes; eight votes had not yet been cast.
Only two of them for us and the day was
ours! The hour had come when, according to law, the polls had to be closed. Every
one looked at the clock and called to the
tardy voters. There came the noise of
tramping in the anteroom; a crowd of eight
people pressed noisily into the hall, at their
head the rough wine dealer, Piepenbrink,

the same one who at the reception recently——

Adel. We know. Tell on——

Send. One after another of the crowd
stepped forward, gave their vote and "Professor Eduard Oldendorf" came out of
each mouth. The last one was this Piepenbrink. Before he cast his vote he asked his
neighbor, "Is the Professor sure to get it?"
"Yes," was the answer. "Then, as the last
elector, I choose for deputy——" (*Pauses.*)

Adel. The Professor?

Send. No. The very shrewd, sly old
fox said, "Dr. Konrad Bolz"—and with
that he turned around shortly and his con-
federates followed him.

Adel. (*Aside, smiling.*) Ah!

Send. Oldendorf is deputy by a majority of two votes!

Col. Well!

Send. It is shameful! No one is to
blame for this outcome but these journalists
on the *Union.* You never saw such a rac-
ing about, such intrigues, such hand-shak--
ing with all the voters, praise for this Oldendorf, and a shrug of the shoulders for
us and for you, honored sir.

Col. So?

Ida. That last is not true!

Adel. (*To Senden.*) Be considerate and
careful here.

Col. You are trembling, my daughter. You are a woman and let such trifles affect you too much. I do not wish to listen to these reports longer. Go, my child! Your friend has won out. There is no reason for you to weep. Help her, Fräulein.

Ida. (*Is led by Adelheid to the side door, left. Beseechingly.*) Leave me! Stay with father!

Send. The bad spirit and the insolence with which this paper is edited are not to be borne longer, on my honor! Colonel, now that we are alone—for Fräulein Adelheid will permit me to number her among us— we have the opportunity of avenging ourselves brilliantly. They have come to the end of their rope. I have already previously sounded the owner of the *Union.* He did not refuse to sell the paper, and only hesitated because of the so-called party which has the sheet in hand at present. The evening of the club party I talked with him myself.

Adel. What do I hear?

Send. This outcome of the election has called forth the greatest bitterness on the part of all our friends, and I do not doubt that, by subscription, we could gather together the purchase price in a few days. That would be a death blow to our opponents, a triumph for the good cause. With the most widely read sheet in the province in our hands, edited by a committee——

Adel. Herr von Senden would not refuse his aid.

Send. It would be my duty to interest myself in it. Colonel, if you would subscribe with us your example would assure the purchase in a moment.

Col. Sir, whatever you wish to do for the furtherance of your political tendencies you are at liberty to do. However, Professor Oldendorf has been a most welcome guest in my house. I shall never work against him behind his back. You might have spared me this hour if, earlier, you had not deceived me with your assurances of the disposition of the majority. I am not angry at you for it. You have acted from the best motives—I am convinced of that. I beg the indulgence of those present if I retire for to-day. I hope to see you again to-morrow, my dear Senden.

Send. Meanwhile I shall prepare the subscription for the purchase of the paper. I take my leave of you. (*Exits.*)

Col. Pardon, Adelheid, for leaving you alone. I wish to write several letters and (*with a forced laugh*) to read my papers.

Adel. (*Sympathetically.*) May I not bear you company just at this time?

Col. (*With an effort.*)   I am better
alone now. (*Exits through centre.*)

Adel. (*Alone.*)   My poor Colonel!
Wounded vanity struggles hard in his true
soul! And Ida? (*Softly opens door at
left, remains standing there.*) She is writing! It is not hard to guess to whom.
(*Closes the door.*) And the evil spirit of
journalism has caused all this mischief!
The whole world complains of him, yet
every one would like to use him for his
own benefit. My Colonel despised newspaper writers for so long till he became
one himself, and Senden lets no opportunity pass to rail at my good friends of the
pen, just in order to step into their places.
I see it coming to this, that Piepenbrink
and I will also become journalists yet, and
together publish a little sheet under the title
Naughty Bolz! So the *Union* is in danger
of being bought secretly? That would be
right beneficial to Konrad. He would then
have to think of other things besides the
newspaper. Oh, the rascal would immediately begin a new one!

(*Enter Oldendorf, Karl, then Ida.*)

Old. (*Still outside the hall.*) And the
Colonel cannot be seen?

Karl. Not by any one, Professor. (*Exits.*)

Adel. (*Opposite Oldendorf.*) Dear

Professor, it is not well that you come just now. We are very much hurt and dissatisfied with the world, more especially with you.

Old. I feared that, but I must speak to him.

Ida. (*Coming towards him from the left door.*) Eduard, I knew that you would come.

Old. My dear Ida! (*Embraces her.*)

Ida. (*On his neck.*) And what is to become of us now?

(*Enter the Colonel.*)

Col. (*Who has entered through centre door, with forced composure.*) You shall not remain in uncertainty about that, my daughter. You, Professor, I beg to forget that you once found friendship in this house; of you (*to Ida*) I ask that you no longer think of the hours when this gentleman told you of his feeling for you. (*More angrily.*) Not one word! In my own house, at least, I shall suffer no attacks from a journalist. Forget him, or forget that you are my daughter! Go in there! (*Leads Ida off, left, without harshness; places himself before the door.*) In this position, Mr. Editor and Deputy, before the heart of my child, you shall not strike me down. (*Exit left.*)

Adel. (*Aside.*) Oh, woe! That is hard!

Old. (*Before the Colonel turns to depart, resolutely.*) Colonel, it is ignoble to refuse me an interview now. (*Goes up to the door.*)

Adel. (*Stepping quickly in his way.*) Stop, no farther! He is in a state of excitement where every word would breed mischief. But do not go from us in this way, Professor—give me just a moment.

Old. I must ask for your forbearance in this mood. I have long feared a similar scene, and I scarcely have strength to preserve my self-control.

Adel. You know our friend, and you know that his quick temper hurries him into unconsidered actions, which he later hastens to set aright.

Old. This is more serious than a whim. It is a break between us—a break which seems irreparable to me.

Adel. Irreparable, Professor? If your feeling for Ida is as I take for granted, then the repair of the breach will not be difficult. Is it not incumbent upon you now, especially now, to yield to her father's wishes? Does not the woman that you love deserve that you sacrifice your ambition for once, at least?

Old. My ambition, yes; my duty, no.

Adel. Your own happiness, Professor, seems to me to be destroyed for a long time, perhaps forever, if you part from Ida in such a way.

Old. (*Gloomily.*) Every one cannot be happy in his private life.

Adel. Such resignation does not please me at all, at least in a man. Pardon me for saying so candidly. (*Good-naturedly.*) Would it be so great an unhappiness, then, if you should not become representative of this city till some years later, or even never?

Old. Fräulein, I am not conceited. I do not estimate my powers very highly, and, as far as I myself can tell, there is no ambitious craving concealed in the bottom of my heart. It is possible that a later age, as you do now, will place a low value on our political contentions, our party strife, and whatever is connected therewith. It is possible that our entire labor will be fruitless. It is possible that the great good which we long for, when it is attained, will be transformed into the opposite; yes, it is highly probable that my own share in the struggle will often be painful, cheerless, and, throughout, not what one could call a remunerative activity; but all that cannot restrain me from devoting my life to the conflicts and controversies of the age to which I belong; for, in spite of all this struggle is the greatest and noblest that the present time will produce. It is not every age that permits its sons to achieve successes that remain great for all time, and, I repeat it, not every century is adapted to making noble and happy the men who live in it.

Adel. I think that every age is adapted to that, if the individuals would be willing to learn how to become efficient and happy. (*Rising.*) You, Professor, are not willing to do anything for the little domestic happiness of your life. You force your friends to act for you.

Old. At least, be as little angry as possible and speak to Ida in my behalf.

Adel. I will try to serve you with my woman's wit, Mr. Statesman. (*Exit Oldendorf.*)

Adel. (*Alone.*) So that is one of the noble, highly educated, free spirits of the German nation! Very rational and extraordinarily virtuous! He would climb into a fire just out of a pure sense of duty! But to win anything, the world, happiness, or, forsooth, a wife—that certainly is not his destiny!

(*Enter Karl.*)

Karl. (*Announcing.*) Dr. Bolz.

Adel. Ah! He, at least, will not be such a paragon of virtue! Where is the Colonel?

Karl. In my lady's room.

Adel. Bring the gentleman in here. (*Exit Karl.*) I feel some embarrassment in seeing you again, Herr Bolz. I must take pains not to show it to you.

(*Enter Bolz.*)

Bolz. A poor soul is just leaving you vainly trying to comfort itself with its philosophy, and now I come, an unhappier one, for yesterday I incurred your displeasure; and without your presence, which cut short a reckless scene, Herr von Senden would have played a bad trick on me in the interests of social propriety. I thank you for the reminder that you gave me. I consider it an indication that you will not withdraw your friendly sympathy from me.

Adel. (*Aside.*) Very artfully, very diplomatically expressed! It is kind of you to interpret my remarkable conduct so charitably. But pardon still another bold interference. That scene with Herr von Senden will not be the occasion for a second?

Bolz. (*Aside.*) Always this Senden!— Your interest in him would be reason enough for me to avoid further consequences. I believe I am able to do it.

Adel. I thank you, and now let me say, you are a dangerous diplomat. You have

effected a complete rout here in the house.
On this evil day just one thing has pleased
me—the single vote that wished to make
you deputy.

Bolz. It was a foolish idea of the good
wine dealer.

Adel. You have taken so much pains to
put your friend through. Why did you
not work for yourself? The young man
whom I once knew had high aims and nothing seemed unattainable to his soaring ambition. Have you changed or does the fire
still burn?

Bolz. (*Smiling.*) I have become a journalist, gracious lady.

Adel. Your friend is one too.

Bolz. Only incidentally. I, however,
belong to the profession. Whoever belongs
to it has ambition to write wittily or
weightily. Whatever goes beyond that is
not for us.

Adel. Not for you?

Bolz. We are too fickle, too restless, too
flighty.

Adel. Are you in earnest, Konrad?

Bolz. Entirely in earnest. Why should
I try to appear different from what I am?
We newspaper writers feed our spirits with
the day's news. We have to taste in suc-
cession, with the tiniest bites, all the dishes
which Satan cooks for mankind; there-

fore you must really make some allowances
for us. The daily vexations over failures
and wickedness, the everlasting little agi-
tations over every possible thing, all that
works on mankind. In the beginning one
clenches his fist; later, however, one becomes accustomed to joke over it. Is it not
natural for one, who works only for the
day, to live only for the passing hour?

Adel. (*Disturbed.*) That is certainly
sad!

Bolz. On the contrary, it is very jolly.
We hum like the bees, fly in spirit through
the whole world, sip the honey wherever we
find it, and sting wherever something dis-
pleases us. Such a life is not exactly made
to produce great heroes, but there must always be queer birds, such as we are.

Adel. (*Aside.*) Now, *he* is beginning,
too, and he is even worse than the other!

Bolz. We will not become sensitive on
that score! I'll write away as long as I am
able. When I give out, then others will
take my place and do the same. When
Konrad Bolz, the grain of wheat, is ground
up in the great mill, then other grains will
fall upon the stones, till the flour is finished, out of which, perhaps, the future
will bake good bread for the benefit of
many.

Adel. No, no! That is fanaticism; such resignation is wrong!

Bolz. Such resignation is found, in the end, in every calling. It is not your lot. Another fortune is due you and you will find it. (*With feeling.*) Adelheid, as a child I wrote you tender verses and lulled myself in foolish dreams. I held you very dear, and the wound which our parting inflicted upon me still pains at times. (*Adelheid makes a deprecatory motion.*) Do not fear. I shall not hurt you. For a long time I begrudged my fate and had hours when I felt like a castaway; but now, as you stand before me in full splendor, so beautiful, so lovable, though my feeling for you is as strong as ever, I must still say: "Your father, to be sure, treated me roughly, but in separating us, in preventing you, the wealthy heiress, accustomed to a life of ease, habituated to exclusive circles, from bestowing your life upon a wild boy, who had always exhibited more arrogance than strength, he was very wise and did exactly right in it."

Adel. (*Grasping his hands in agitation.*) I thank you, Konrad; I thank you for speaking thus of my dead father. Yes, you are good, you have a heart. Your showing me that makes me very happy.

Bolz. It is only a very small, pocket

edition of a heart for private use. Its appearance, thus, was against my will.

Adel. And now enough of us two. Here in this house there is need of our assistance. You have won, you have carried your wishes through, entirely contrary to ours. I submit and acknowledge you as my master. Now, however, be merciful, and become my ally. In this conflict of men the heart of a maiden that I love has been deeply wounded. I would like to heal it, and wish that you would help me.

Bolz. Command me.

Adel. The Colonel must be propitiated. Think up something that is efficacious in healing wounded vanity.

Bolz. I have thought of that and have prepared something. Unfortunately, I can do nothing but make him realize that his anger towards Oldendorf is nonsense. You, alone, can summon the gentle spirit which impels to reconciliation.

Adel. Then we women will have to work out our own salvation.

Bolz. Meanwhile I hasten to do the little that I am able.

Adel. Farewell, Herr Editor. Do not ponder the course of the great world alone, but think at times also of a lonely friend, who suffers from the unworthy selfishness of seeking happiness on her own account.

Bolz.   You have always found your happiness in caring for the happiness of others. Whoever has that sort of selfishness, for him it is an easy matter to be happy. (*Exit Bolz.*)

Adel. (*Alone.*)   He loves me yet! He is a high-minded, tender-hearted man! But even he is resigned! They are all sick, these men! They have no courage! Out of sheer learning and brooding over themselves they have lost confidence in themselves. This Konrad! Why does he not say to me, "Adelheid, I want you for my wife." He used to be shameless enough! But no! He must needs philosophize over my sort of happiness and his sort of happiness! It was all very beautiful, but it is stupid stuff! There in the country my young squires are a different sort of people, I tell you. They do not carry any large bundle of wisdom around with them, and they have more whims and prejudices· than are pardonable; but they hate and love away vigorously and defiantly, and never forget to look out for their own interests. They are better off for it. Commend me to the country, the fresh air and the fields! (*Pause. With determination.*) The *Union* is to be sold. Konrad *shall* go to the country, so that he may forget his vagaries. (*Sits down and writes. Rings.*)

(*Enter Karl.*)

This letter goes to Lawyer Schwarz. I beg him to come to me on a pressing matter of business.

(*Enter Ida.*)

Ida. (*Comes through the side door, left.*) Restlessly, I wander around! Let me cry it out here? (*Weeps on Adelheid's neck.*)

Adel. (*Tenderly.*) Poor child! The wicked men have treated you cruelly! Mourn if you wish, darling, but do not be so silent and submissive!

Ida. I have only the one thought—he is lost to me, lost forever!

Adel. You are my good girl. But be calm! You have not lost him at all. On the contrary, we will see to it that you get him back, handsomer than ever. With blushing cheeks and beaming eyes, he shall step before you again, the noble man, your chosen demigod, and the demigod shall implore your forgiveness for having caused you pain.

Ida. (*Stepping up to her.*) What are you saying?

Adel. Listen! To-night I read in the stars that you were to be the wife of a representative. A large star fell from heaven and upon it in legible letters was written, ''Unquestionably, she shall have him!'' The fulfillment depends only upon one condition.

Ida. What condition? Tell me!

Adel. I told you recently about a certain young lady and an unknown gentleman. You remember?

Ida. I have been thinking about it incessantly.

Adel. On the same day that this lady recovers her knight you will be reconciled to your Professor. Not earlier, not later— thus it stands written.

Ida. I believe you gladly. And when will this day come?

Adel. Well, sweetheart, I don't exactly know; but, in confidence, because we girls are alone, the aforesaid lady is thoroughly tired of the long hoping and waiting and I fear that she will take a desperate step.

Ida. (*Embracing her.*) Only see that it isn't too long in coming.

Adel. (*Holding her.*) Hush! Be sure that not a man hears us!

(*Enter Korb.*)

What is it, old friend?

Korb. Outside is Herr Bellmaus, the friend——

Adel. Very well. And he wishes to speak to me?

Korb. Yes. I myself urged him to apply to you. He has something to tell you.

Adel. Bring him in! (*Exit Korb.*)

Ida. Let me go. My eyes are red and swollen.

Adel. Go then, my dear. I shall be with you in a few moments. (*Exit Ida.*)

And now *he* is here! The whole *Union*, one after another!

(*Enter Bellmaus.*)

Bell. (*Timidly and with many bows.*) You gave me permission, gracious lady——

Adel. (*Kindly.*) I am glad to see you here at my house, and I am curious regarding the interesting disclosures which you are about to make to me.

Bell. I would confide what I have heard to no one more gladly than to yourself, gracious lady. When I learned from Herr Korb that you were a subscriber to our paper, then I was positive——

Adel. That I deserved to be a friend of the editor. Thanks for the compliment.

Bell. There is this Schmock! He is a poor man who has mingled but little in good society and was, until now, associate editor of the *Coriolanus.*

Adel. I remember having seen him.

Bell. I gave him several glasses of punch, at the request of Bolz. Thereupon he grew merry and told me of a great con-

spiracy between Senden and the editor of
the *Coriolanus*. These two gentlemen, according to his assertion, planned to bring
our Professor Oldendorf into disrepute
with the Colonel, and for that reason they
induced the latter to write articles in the
Coriolanus.

Adel. Is the young man at all reliable
who made these revelations to you?

Bell. He cannot stand much punch and
when he had drunk three glasses he related
all this to me voluntarily. Otherwise, I do
not consider him so very reliable, of course.
I believe he is a good fellow, but reliable?
No, he isn't that.

Adel. (*Indifferently.*) Would this man
—who drank the three glasses of punch—
be prepared to repeat his disclosures before
other people, do you suppose?

Bell. He told me that he would, and
also spoke of proofs.

Adel. (*Aside.*) Ah! (*Aloud.*) I fear
the proofs would not be sufficient. And
you have made no statement to the Professor or to Herr Bolz about this?

Bell. Our Professor is very much oc-
cupied just now, and Bolz is the best and
most jovial man in the world, but since his
relations with Herr von Senden are already
strained without this, I thought——

Adel. (*Quickly.*) And you were quite

right, dear Herr Bellmaus. Then otherwise you are satisfied with Herr Bolz?

Bell. He is a sociable and splendid man and I stand on very good terms with him—we all stand on very good terms with him.

Adel. I am glad.

Bell. Occasionally he is a trifle overbearing, but he has the best heart in the world.

Adel. (*Aside.*) Out of the mouths of babes and sucklings shall ye hear the truth!

Bell. To be sure, he has a purely prosaic nature. He has no soul for poetry.

Adel. Do you think so?

Bell. Yes. He frequently gets sarcastic about it.

Adel. (*Bringing the interview to a close.*) I thank you for your information, even if I cannot attach any weight to it, and I am glad to have become acquainted in you with a part of the editorial staff. Journalists, I notice, are dangerous people, and it is well to keep their good will, although I, as an insignificant personage, will endeavor never to give material for a newspaper article. (*As Bellmaus hesitates about going.*) Can I serve you in any other way?

Bell. (*Warmly.*) Yes, gracious lady, if you will have the goodness to accept this copy of my poems. They are only poems of youth, my first attempts, but I count upon your kind indulgence. (*Draws a gilt-edged book out of his pocket and hands it to her.*)

Adel. Thank you sincerely, Herr Bellmaus. Never before has a poet presented his works to me. I shall read the beautiful book through in the country, and under my trees rejoice that I have friends in the city who think of me also when they portray the beautiful for others.

Bell. (*Fervently.*) Rest assured, gracious lady, that no poet will ever forget you who has had the good fortune of knowing you. (*Exits with a deep bow.*)

Adel. (*Alone.*) This Herr Schmock with his three glasses of punch is well worth an acquaintance. Korb shall look him up at once. I have scarcely arrived in the city, and yet my room is like a business office, in which editors and authors are plying their trades. I fear that is an omen. (*Exit left.*)

(*It grows dark. Enter Colonel from garden.*)

Col. (*Coming slowly forward.*) I am glad that it is all over between us. (*Stamping his foot.*) I am very glad! (*Despondently.*) I feel free and easy, as I have not for a long time. I believe I could sing. At this moment I am the subject of conversation at all the tea-tables, on all the ale-house benches. Everywhere chatter and laughter: ''Serves him right, the old fool!'' Confound it!

(*Enter Karl, with lights and papers.*)

Who told you that you could bring the lights?

Karl. Colonel, it is the hour when you are accustomed to read the paper. Here it is. (*Lays it on the table.*)

Col. Worthless people, these men of the pen! Cowardly, malicious, insidious in their anonymous attacks! How these crews will exult now! And over me! How they will exalt their editor way to the clouds! There lies the contemptible sheet! In it is my defeat, trumpeted forth with cheeks blown out, with scornful shrugs of the shoulders—away with it! (*Walks up and down, looks at the paper on the floor, picks it up.*) I will drink to the dregs! (*Sits down.*) Right here at the beginning! (*Reading.*) ''Professor Oldendorf—majority of two votes. This paper is bound to rejoice over the result.'' I believe that. ''But not less gratifying was the contest that preceded it.'' Naturally. ''Perhaps it has never occurred before that, as here, there were opposed to each other two men, so closely bound by an enduring friendship, both alike distinguished by the good will of

their fellow citizens. It was a chivalrous
race between two friends, full of generosity,
without animosity, without jealousy. It is
even possible that hidden in the heart of
each of them was the wish that his friendly
opponent, and not himself, might be the
victor.'' (*Lays aside the sheet, wipes his
brow.*) What kind of talk is that? (*Reads.*)
''And, putting aside all party prejudice,
no man has ever been more entitled to the
victory than our honored opponent. This
is not the place to boast of what his value is
to his large circle of friends, on account of
his straightforward, noble personality; but
the way he has labored by word and deed,
through his active interest in all the city's
measures for the public good, is known generally, and appreciated to-day with lively
gratitude by our fellow citizens.'' (*Lays
aside the sheet.*) That is a mean style!
(*Reads further.*) ''By a very small majority of votes our city has decided to support in the Chamber the political principles
of the younger friend, but addresses and
delegations have been made ready to-day,
as rumored, by all parties, not to fete the
victor in the struggle, but to express to his
rival, his noble friend, the universal respect
and esteem, of which there never was a man
more worthy than he.'' That is open assassination! That is a fearful imprudence in

Oldendorf! That is a journalist's revenge,
so delicate and so pointed! Oh, that seems
like him! No, that doesn't seem like him!
It is revolting, it is inhuman! What am I
to do? Delegations and addresses for me?
For Oldendorf's friend? Bah! That is all
gossip, newspaper gabble, that costs nothing but a few words! The city knows nothing of these sensations. It is a piece of
knavery.

(Enter Karl.)

Karl. Letters from the post office.
(Lays them on the able. Exits.)

Col. There is still more in them.   I
shrink from opening them.   *(Breaks the
seal of the first.)*   What the devil!   A
poem, and to me? "To our noble political
opponent, the finest man of the city."
Signed? What is the signature? Baus!
Baus? Baus? I do not know it. It must
be a pseudonym. *(Reads.)* It seems to be
capital poetry! And what is here? *(Opens
second letter.)* "To the benefactor of the
poor, to the father of the orphaned," an
address— *(Reads.)* "Honor and good-
will,"—Signature, "many women and
maidens," the seal a P.P.? Heavens! What
is the meaning of all this? Am I be-
witched? If they are in truth voices from
the city and if this day is thus understood
by the people, then I must confess that the

people think better of me—than I myself.
(Enter Karl.)

Karl. A number of men wish to speak to the Colonel.

Col. What kind of men?

Karl. They say a delegation of voters.

Col. Bring them in. This damned newspaper was right, after all.

(<i>Enter Piepenbrink, Kleinmichel and three other men. They bow, the Colonel does likewise.</i>)

Piep. (<i>Solemnly.</i>) My dear Colonel! A number of voters have sent us to you as a delegation to tell you that the entire city considers you an eminently excellent and upright man.

Col. (<i>Stiffly.</i>) I am grateful for the compliment.

Piep. It isn't anything to be grateful for. It is the truth. You are an honorable man, through and through, and it gives us pleasure to tell you so. It cannot be disagreeable to you to hear this from your fellow citizens.

Col. I have always regarded myself as a man of honor, gentlemen.

Piep. There you are just right, and you have also proven your very good character at every opportunity. With poverty, with famine, in guardianships, also at our rifle match, everywhere that a benevolent and good man could be useful to and give pleasure to us citizens, there you have been foremost. Always unpretentious and truehearted, without swagger and haughtiness. Thus it comes that we all love and honor you.

Col. (*Passes his hand over his eyes.*)

Piep. To-day many of us voted for the Professor, many on account of politics, many because they knew that he was your particular friend, and perhaps will be your son-in-law.

Col. (*Without harshness.*) Sir——

Piep. I did not vote for you myself.

Col. (*Somewhat more emphatically.*) Sir——

Piep. But for that very reason I come to you with the others, and for that very reason we are telling you how you are thought of in this community; and we all wish that you may still preserve, for a long time, your manly views and your friendly heart for us, as an honored, extremely fine gentleman and fellow citizen.

Col. (*Without harshness.*) Why do you not say this to the Professor on whom your choice has fallen?

Piep. He is young yet. He must first earn the city's thanks in the Chamber. You, however, have earned it at our hands and therefore we come to you.

Col. (*Sincerely.*) I thank you, sir, for your friendly words. Just at present they are especially agreeable to me. I ask your name.

Piep. I am called Piepenbrink.

Col. (*Coolly, but not discourteously.*) Oh, so? That is the name. (*With reserve.*) I thank you, gentlemen, for the kindly opinion you have expressed, no matter whether you represent the true sentiment of the city or whether you are speaking at the request of individuals. I thank you and I shall continue to do what I believe to be right. (*Bows, the delegation does likewise. Exeunt the latter.*) So that is this Piepenbrink—the warm friend of his friend! But this man's words were intelligent, and his whole appearance respectable. It is impossible that all of that can be trickery. Who knows! There are clever schemers. To send newspaper articles, letters, and these good-hearted people into my house in order to soften me, to pass as my friends before all the world, in order to force me to trust in their falseness again! Yes, so it is. It is a put-up scheme! They'll find they are mistaken.

(*Enter Karl.*)

Karl. Dr. Bolz.

Col. I am at home to no more people!

Karl. I told the gentleman that, but he

insisted on speaking to the Colonel. He says he comes on an affair of honor.

Col. What? Oldendorf will surely not be so insane—bring him in.

(*Enter Bolz.*)

Bolz. (*With dignity.*) Colonel, I have come to make an announcement to you which the honor of a third makes necessary.

Col. I am prepared for it, and beg you not to protract it too long.

Bolz. Only as long as is necessary. The article in this evening's issue of the *Union* which discusses your personality was written by me without Oldendorf's knowledge.

Col. It is scarcely of interest to me to know who wrote the article.

Bolz. (*Courteously.*) But it is of importance to me to tell you that it is not by Oldendorf, and that Oldendorf knew nothing of it. During these last weeks my friend was so lost in the sadness and pain which he had to endure that he left the management of the paper to me alone. I myself am answerable for everything that it has contained recently.

Col. To what end are you making this confession?

Bolz. It will not escape your perception, Colonel, that after the scene that took place to-day between you and my friend, Oldendorf, as a man of honor, could neither write such an article nor publish it in his paper.

Col. How so, sir? In the article itself I have found nothing reprehensible.

Bolz. In your eyes the article exposes my friend to the suspicion of trying, by shameless flattery, to regain your sympathy. Nothing is farther from him than such a course. You, Colonel, are too much a man of honor yourself to consider natural mean-spirited actions with an enemy.

Col. You are right. (*Aside.*) This insolence is unbearable! Is your explanation at an end?

Bolz. It is. I have a second one to add to it—namely, that I myself regret very much having written this article.

Col. I surely do you no injustice in assuming that you have already written other things which were to be regretted.

Bolz. (*Continuing.*) I had this article published before your last conversation with Oldendorf came to my knowledge. (*Very courteously.*) I regret it because it is not quite true. I was too hasty when I portrayed your personality to the public. The picture, to-day at least, no longer corresponds to the truth. It is flattery.

Col. (*Interrupting.*) Now, by the devil, that is enough!

Bolz. Pardon, but it is true. I wish to

convince you that even a journalist can regret having written untruth.

Col. Sir. (*Aside.*) I must control myself, else he will keep the right on his side. Doctor, I see that you are an adroit man, and understand your trade. Since, moreover, you seem in the mood to-day to speak only the truth, I request you further to tell me whether, perhaps, you have led the demonstrations which were represented to me to-day to be the voice of the public.

Bolz. (*Bowing.*) I grant that I have not been inactive in that connection.

Col. (*Extending the letters to him, angrily.*) Have you instigated this?

Bolz. In part, Colonel. The poem is the outpouring of an honest youth's heart, who honors, in you, Oldendorf's fatherly friend, and his ideal of a chivalrous hero. I encouraged him to send it to you. It at least was well meant. The poet will have to seek another ideal. The address comes from women and children who constitute the Society for the Education of Destitute Children. The Society numbers even Fräulein Ida Berg among its numbers. I myself drew up this address for the ladies. It was transcribed by the daughter of the wine dealer, Piepenbrink.

Col. That is about the way I had judged these letters. It is unnecessary to ask whether you are the engineer who drove the citizens here to me.

Bolz. At least I did not dissuade them.
*(From without a male chorus of many
voices.)*

"Hurrah, Hurrah, Hurrah!
Within the confines of our walls
    There dwells a noble knight;
And this true-hearted man is blessed
    By every burgher's wight.
Whoe'er seeks aid in need, bespeaks
    His goodness, untoward.
His coat-of-mail is formed of LOVE,
    Of SYMPATHY, his sword.
To-day we fete, with speech and song,
The one who rights the poor man's
        wrong.
    The Colonel, the Colonel,
        Our noble Colonel Berg."

Col. (*Rings after the first measures of
the song.*)

(Enter Karl.)

Col. You will admit no one, if you wish to remain in my service.

Karl. (*Frightened.*) Colonel, they are in the garden already, a great company. It is the choral club; the leaders are even now standing upon the steps.

Bolz. (*Who has opened the window.*) Very well sung, Colonel. "Templar and Jewess." It is the best tenor of our city

and the accompaniment is quite original.

Col. (*Aside.*) It is enough to drive one mad! Bring the gentlemen in. (*Exit Karl at the end of the stanza; enter Fritz Kleinmichel and two other men.*)

Fritz. Colonel, the local choral club asks permission to sing you some songs. Kindly consider the serenade as a slight expression of the universal respect and love.

Col. Gentlemen, I regret very much that illness in my family will make it desirable that you curtail your artistic performances. I thank you for your good intentions and beg you to sing to Professor Oldendorf the songs which you intended for me.

Fritz. We considered it our duty to pay our respects to you first before looking up your friend. In order not to disturb the sick, we shall, with your permission, take our stand farther from the house in the garden.

Col. Do as you please. (*Fritz and the other two exeunt.*) Is this procession also at your instigation?

Bolz. (*Bowing.*) At least in part. But you are too kind, Colonel, when you attribute all these demonstrations to me alone. My share in them is very small. I have done nothing but guide public opinion a little bit. These numerous people are not puppets, whom a skilful puppet-player may pull about on their wires. All these voices belong to efficient and worthy persons, and whatever they have said to you is, indeed, the general sentiment of the city; that is, the conviction of the better and more intelligent part of the city. Were it not so, I would have toiled in vain with these good people to lead even one of them into your house.

Col. (*Aside.*) He is right again, and I am always in the wrong.

Bolz. (*Very politely.*) Permit me the further explanation that even these delicate manifestations of universal regard seem to me to be unbecoming at the present time, and that I regret deeply the part that I have taken in them. To-day, at least, a friend of Oldendorf's has no cause to do honor to your chivalrous spirit or your self-denial.

Col. (*Going towards him.*) Doctor, you avail yourself of the privilege of your profession to speak without reserve and to insult strangers in a way that exhausts my patience. You are in my house, and it is a customary consideration of social propriety to respect the privacy of one's opponent.

Bolz. (*Leaning over a chair, pleasantly.*) If you mean by that that you possess the right to put out of your house unwelcome strangers, then it was unnecessary to remind me of it, for already to-day you have turned out of your house another whose love for you gave him a greater right to be here than I have.

Col. Sir, such barefaced effrontery has never before come to my notice.

Bolz. (*Bowing.*) I am a journalist, Colonel, and only lay claim to what you have just called the privilege of my profession.

(*March by wind instruments. Karl comes in quickly.*)

Col. (*To him.*) Lock the garden gate. There shall no one come in! (*The music ceases.*)

Bolz. (*At window.*) You are shutting out your friends. This time I am guiltless.

Karl. Oh, Colonel, it is too late. Back there in the garden the singers are standing and in front there is a tremendous procession marching before the house. It is Herr von Senden and the whole club. (*Retires to back of stage.*)

Col. Sir, I wish this discussion between us to end.

Bolz. (*Answering back from the window.*) Considering your position, Colonel, I find that wish quite natural. (*Looking out again.*) A brilliant procession. They are all carrying paper lanterns. On the lanterns are inscriptions. Besides the usual mottoes of the club I see still another. Why is it that Bellmaus is never around when he could be of use to the paper! (*Quickly drawing out a pocketbook.*) We will jot the inscriptions down rapidly for the paper. (*Speaking over his shoulder.*) Pardon! Oh, that is highly remarkable: ''Down with our enemies!'' and here: a blackish lantern with white letters: ''Perish the *Union!*'' Hang it! (*Calling out of the window.*) Good evening, gentlemen!

Col. (*Stepping up to him.*) Sir, you are the devil's own!

Bolz. (*Turning around suddenly.*) It is good of you, Colonel, to show yourself beside me in the window. (*Col. steps back.*)

Send. (*From below.*) What voice is that?

Bolz. Good evening, Herr von Senden. The gentleman who carries the brown lantern with the white inscription would oblige us greatly if he would have the goodness to hand the lantern up to the Colonel. Blow out your light, man, and hand me the lantern. So. I thank you, Man-with-the-witty-motto. (*Bringing in the lantern on a pole.*) Here, Colonel, is the written proof of the brotherly feelings which your friends entertain towards us. (*Wrenches the lantern from the pole.*) The lantern for you, the pole for the bearer. (*Throws the pole out of the window.*) I have the honor to take my leave. (*Turns to go. Meets Adelheid.*)

(*Male chorus nearer again, "There is a highly honored knight." Flourish of trumpets. Many voices, "Long live Colonel Berg! Hurrah!"*)

Adel. (*Entering from left side, during noise.*) Is the whole town in a riot to-day?

Bolz. I have done my part. He is half converted. Good night!

Col. (*Throwing lantern on the ground, raging.*) To the devil with all journalists!

(*Male chorus, Senden, Blumenberg and many other men in procession, visible at garden gate. The delegation enters, chorus with lanterns; they group themselves at the entrance.*)

Send. (*In loud voice, till the curtain is down.*) Colonel, the club gives itself the honor of paying its respects to its highly esteemed member. (*Curtain falls during the last words.*)

FOURTH ACT

SCENE: Summer parlor in the Colonel's house.

(*Colonel entering from garden, behind him Karl.*)

Col. (*At entrance, crossly.*) Who ordered William to lead the horse around in front of my bedroom? The rascal makes noise enough with his hoofs to wake the dead.

Karl. Isn't the Colonel going to ride out to-day?

Col. No! To the stable with the horse!

Karl. As you order, sir. (*Exit.*)

Col. (*Rings. Karl again at the door.*) Is the Fräulein to be seen?

Karl. She is in her room. The Herr Justizrat has been with her already an hour.

Col. What! So early in the morning?

Karl. Here she is herself. (*Exits after Adelheid has entered.*)

(*Enter Adelheid, Korb, from door at right.*)

Adel. (*To Korb.*) Just stay near the

136

garden door, and if the aforesaid young gentleman comes, bring him to us. (*Exit Korb.*) Good morning, Colonel. (*Approaching him and looking at him brightly.*) How is the weather to-day?

Col. Cloudy, girl, cloudy and stormy. Anger and grief buzz around in my head till it is like to fly to pieces. How is the little one?

Adel. Better. She was sensible enough to go to sleep towards morning. Now she is sad, but composed.

Col. This very composure vexes me. If she would only scream once in awhile, or tear her hair a little! It would be terrifying, but it would be more natural. But this smiling and turning away, this drying secret tears—that takes all my self-control from me. It is very unnatural in my child.

Adel. Perhaps she knows her father's kind heart better than he does himself. Perhaps she is still hoping.

Col. For what? For a reconciliation with him? After what has happened a reconciliation between Oldendorf and myself is impossible.

Adel. (*Aside.*) I wonder if he wants me to contradict him.

(*Enter Korb.*)

Korb. (*To Adelheid.*) The man has come.

Adel. I will **ring.** (*Exit Korb.*) Help me in a little dilemma. I have to talk with a strange young man who seems in need of assistance, and I would like you to stay in the vicinity—may I leave the door open here? (*Points to door at left.*)

Col. I suppose that means, in plain language, that I am to go in there?

Adel. Only for five minutes, please.

Col. I don't mind, as long as I don't have to listen.

Adel. I do not ask that, but listen you will, if the conversation should interest you.

Col. (*Smiling.*) Then I shall come in. (*Exits left. Adelheid rings.*) (*Enter Schmock. Korb at entrance, exits again immediately.*)

Schmock. (*Bowing.*) I wish you good morning. Are you the young lady who sent her secretary to me?

Adel. Yes. You expressed a wish to talk to me yourself.

Schmock. How does the secretary know when I have something to say to you? Here are the scraps of paper which Senden wrote and which I found in the waste basket of the *Coriolanus.* Look and see whether they are of use to the Colonel. What can I start with them? There is nothing to be done.

Adel. (*Looking on, reading aside.*) "I herewith send you the unhappy specimen of composition," and so forth. Unguarded and very ordinary! (*Lays them on table. Aloud.*) In any case, these insignificant notes are better in my waste basket than in another's. And what causes you, sir, to give me your confidence?

Schmock. Bellmaus told me that you were a clever person, who would tell the Colonel tactfully that he should be on his guard against my editor and Senden; and the Colonel is a humane man. Recently he offered me a glass of sweet wine and a roll with salmon for breakfast.

Col. (*Visible at the door, folding his hands compassionately.*) Dear God!

Schmock. Why should I let him be taken in by these men?

Adel. If that breakfast was not distasteful to you, we will provide for another one.

Schmock. Oh, please do not trouble yourself on my account.

Adel. Can we help you in anything else?

Schmock. In what should you help me? (*Examining his boots and clothes.*) I have everything in good repair now. My only misfortune is that I am stuck in a bad business. I must see that I get out of literature.

Adel. (*Sympathetically.*) It is very hard, then, to get along well in literature?

Schmock. That depends. My editor is

an unjust man. He strikes out too much
and pays too little. "Consider your style,
above everything," he says. "Good style
is the main thing. Write impressively,
Schmock," he says; "write deep! These
days, one demands of a newspaper that it
be deep." Good. I write deep, I make my
style logical, but when I bring him my
work, he throws it from him and shrieks,
"What is that? That is heavy, that is pe-
dantic," he says. "You must write wittily,
you must be brilliant, Schmock. It is the
fashion now for everything to be pleasing
to the reader." What am I to do? I write
again, wittily. I put much brilliance into
the article, and when I bring it he takes his
red pencil and strikes out everything common and leaves in it only the brilliant part.

Col. Is such a thing possible?

Schmock. How can I live with such
treatment? How can I write nothing but
brilliant things for him at five pfennigs
a line? I cannot live on that, and, therefore, I will see to it that I get out of the
business. If I could only earn twenty-five
or thirty thalers I would never write for a
newspaper again in my life. I would start
my own business, a little business that
could support me.

Adel. Wait a moment. (*Hunts around
in her purse.*)

Col. (*Hastening forward.*) Permit me,
dear Adelheid. The young man wishes to
leave journalism. That is a matter for me.
Here, here is money, as you wish, if you
promise me never to touch a pen again for
a periodical from this day forward. Here,
take it!

Schmock. A Prussian banknote for
twenty-five thalers currency? On my hon-
or I promise you, Colonel, on my honor and
salvation I go this very day to a cousin of
mine who has a sound business. Does the
Colonel wish a duebill or shall I draw up a
long-term draft on myself?

Col. Keep away from me with your
draft!

Schmock. Then I will draw up a duebill.
I prefer that it be only a duebill.

Col. (*Impatiently.*) Even your duebill
I do not want. Sir, in God's name, go!

Schmock. But how will it be about the
interest? If I can have it at five per cent.
it would please me.

Adel. The gentleman is giving you the
money.

Schmock. He is giving me the money?
It is a miracle! I tell you, Colonel, if I do
not make anything with the money, it will
have to remain a gift; but if I get on my
feet with it, then I'll return it to you. I
hope that I may get on my feet.

Col. Arrange that just as you see fit.

Schmock. It is entirely satisfactory to me so, Colonel. Meanwhile I thank you, and hope you may be repaid by other joys which you have. I take my leave of you, my lady and gentleman.

Adel. We will not forget about the breakfast. (*Rings. Enter Korb.*) Dear Korb! (*Talks with him softly.*)

Schmock. Thanks, very much. Let it be so! (*Exeunt Schmock and Korb.*)

Col. And now, my lady, explain this whole interview to me. It concerns me closely enough.

Adel. Senden has indiscreetly spoken his mind to others about his relations with you and your household. This young man had heard something of it and had in his possession notes from Senden, in which were several unwarrantable expressions. I considered it wise to get these notes out of his hands.

Col. I ask you for these letters, Adelheid.

Adel. (*Pleadingly.*) For what, Colonel?

Col. I shall not become angry, girl.

Adel. It would not be worth your while; and yet I beg you not to look in them. You know enough now, for you know that he, with his associates, is not worthy of such great trust as you have granted him of late.

Col. (*Sadly.*)   Oh, fie, fie! I am unfortunate in my friends in my old age.

Adel. If you put Oldendorf in a class with these (*points to the letters*), you are wrong.

Col. That I do not do, girl. Senden I have not loved as much, and therefore it is easier to stand his injuring me.

Adel. (*Gently.*) And because you loved the other one was the reason, yesterday, that you were so——

Col. Say it right out, moralist—so hard and violent.

Adel. More than that. You were unjust.

Col. I said the same thing last night, when I stepped to Ida's room and heard the poor thing weeping. I was a wounded, angry man and was wrong in the form; but in the matter itself I was quite right. Let him be deputy. He is better fitted for it, perhaps, than I; but the fact that he is a newspaper writer separates us.

Adel. He is only doing what you did also.

Col. Do not remind me of that foolishness! If he, as my son-in-law, judged the course of the world differently than I, I could, no doubt, endure it easily. If he,

however, shouts loudly out into the world,
every day, sentiments and principles which
are opposed to mine, and I have to read
them and have to hear everywhere how my
son-in-law is derided and abused by my
friends and old comrades on that account
and I have to swallow it all—you see, I
cannot do it.

Adel. And Ida? Because you cannot
bear that therefore Ida must become unhappy.

Col. My poor child! She has been unhappy through this entire period. This
half-hearted association between us men has
long been a bad thing. It is better that it
come to an end, though with great pain.

Adel. (*Earnestly.*) I do not see the
end yet. I shall not see it till Ida laughs
as merrily as she was wont to do.

Col. (*Excitedly marching around;
bursting out.*) So I am to give my child
over to him and seat myself in a corner
alone! I pictured my last days differently,
but God forbid that my beloved girl should
become unhappy through me. He is reliable and honorable and will care for her
well, and I will return to the little city
from which I came hither.

Adel. (*Grasping his hand.*) My worthy
friend, no! That you are not to do.
Neither Oldendorf nor Ida would wish to

owe their happiness to such a sacrifice. If Senden, now, and his friends should take the paper out of the Professor's hands, what then?

Col. (*Joyfully.*) Then he would no longer be a journalist! (*Uneasily.*) I will hear nothing of the plan. These underhanded actions do not please me.

Adel. Nor me either. (*Heartily.*) Colonel, you have often shown a confidence in me that has made me proud and happy. Just to-day you allowed me to speak more freely than is usually permitted a girl. Will you give me still another great proof of your esteem?

Col. (*Pressing her hand.*) Adelheid, we know how we stand with each other. Speak!

Adel. Be my true knight to-day, for an hour. Permit me to lead you whithersoever it may happen.

Col. What have you in mind, child?

Adel. Nothing wrong, nothing that would be beneath your dignity or mine. It is not to remain a secret from you long.

Col. If it must be, I surrender. But may I not at least know what I have to do?

Adel. You are to accompany me on a call and, in connection, not to forget what we have just spoken of so sensibly.

Col. On a call?

(*Enter Korb.*)

Adel. On a call which I am making in my own interest.

Korb. (*To Adel.*) Herr von Senden wishes to pay his respects to you.

Col. I will not see him, now.

Adel. Careful, Colonel. We haven't time to be angry, even with him. I shall be obliged to receive him for a few minutes.

Col. Then I leave.

Adel. (*Entreatingly.*) To accompany me at once? The carriage is waiting.

Col. I obey the command. (*Exits left.*)

Adel. I have made up my mind hastily, I have ventured something that was much too bold for a girl, for I feel now that my courage is leaving me as the crisis is approaching. I must do it for his sake and for us all! (*To Korb.*) Ask Fräulein Ida to be ready. The coachman is to return immediately to fetch her. Dear Korb! Think of me. I am going on an important errand, my old friend. (*Exit Adelheid.*)

Korb. (*Alone.*) Goodness! How her eyes shine! What is she about? She surely isn't going to elope with the old Colonel? Whatever she is up to, she will carry it through. There is only one person who could get the upper hand of her. Oh, Herr Konrad! If I only dared speak! (*Exits.*)

SCENE: Editorial office of the *Union*.
(*Bolz enters from door at left, Müller immediately after.*)

Bolz. (*At centre door.*)   Come in with the table!

Müller. (*Carrying a small table covered with wine bottles, glasses and plates to the front, at left. Draws up five chairs. Speaks.*)   Herr Piepenbrink presents his compliments and says the wine is some of the yellow seal, and if the Doctor should drink toasts, he hopes he will not forget Herr Piepenbrink's health.   He was very jolly, the fat little man!   And Madame Piepenbrink reminded him that he was to subscribe to the *Union*.   He commissioned me to order it.

Bolz. (*Who meantime has been rummaging in the papers. Rising.*)   Bring the wine! (*Müller pours out a glass.*)   In honor of the worthy vintner! (*Drinks.*)   I trifled with him inconsiderately, but his heart has proven itself to be true.   Tell him the health has not been forgotten.   Here is a bottle for you!   Now, take yourself off!
(*Exit Müller. Bolz opening door at left.*)
Come, gentlemen, to-day I redeem my agreement.

(*Enter Kämpe, Bellmaus, Körner.*)

Here is the promised breakfast. And now, my dearest ephemera, quick! Paint your cheeks and your humor as rose-colored as is possible to your wits. (*Filling his glass.*) The great victory is won; the *Union* has celebrated one of the noblest of triumphs. In coming centuries belated grandchildren will say in astonishment: "Those were glorious days," and so forth. For continuation, see to-day's issue of the paper! Before we sit down, the first toast.

Kämpe. The deputy-elect!

Bolz. No, the first toast belongs to the common mother, the great power which brings forth deputies—The Newspaper! Long may it flourish!

All. Hurrah!

(*They touch glasses.*)

Bolz. Hurrah! And for the second, long live—wait! The deputy himself is missing!

Kämpe. There he comes!

(*Enter Oldendorf*)

Bolz. The representative of our honored city, editor-in-chief and Professor, journalist and excellent man, who is actually wrathful, just at present, because indiscretions have been put in the paper behind his back—long may he live!

All. Hurrah!

Old. (*Pleasantly.*) I thank you, gentlemen.

Bolz. (*Drawing Oldendorf forward, aside.*) And you are no longer angry?

Old. Your intentions were good, but it was a great imprudence.

Bolz. Don't think of it any more. (*Aloud.*) Here, take the glass, sit down with us! Don't be proud, young statesman! To-day you belong to us. So—here sits the staff! Where is the worthy Herr Henning? Where is the owner, printer and publisher, Gabriel Henning?

Bell. We have looked for him everywhere. He is nowhere to be found.

Kämpe. I met him awhile ago on the stairs. He slipped by me as timorously as some one who had been guilty of a stupid trick.

Bolz. Probably it is with him as with Oldendorf. He is dissatisfied again with the views of the paper.

(*Enter Müller.*)

Müller. (*Putting his head in.*) Here is the mail—and the papers.

Bolz. Come in! (*Müller steps in, lays the papers on the table.*)

Müller. Here is the *Coriolanus.* There is something in it about our paper. The *Coriolanus* messenger boy grinned scornfully at me and recommended the article to me for perusal.

Bolz. Give it to me! Be still, O Roman people! Coriolanus speaks! The devil! What is this? (*Reads.*) "We have just learned from the best sources that a great change is imminent in the newspaper life of our province. Our rival, the *Union*, will cease its unbridled attacks on all that is high and holy." This high and holy means Blumenberg. "The proprietorship of the same is to be transferred into other hands, and there is a safe prospect that from now on we will welcome an ally in this much-read sheet." How does that sound, gentlemen?

Müller. Confound it! ⎫
Kämpe. That is nonsense! ⎬ (*Together.*)
Bell. It is a lie! ⎭

Old. That is another of Blumenberg's fantastic inventions.

Bolz. There is something behind this. Bring Gabriel Henning to me! (*Exit Müller.*) This proprietor has played traitor; we are poisoned! (*Springing up.*) And this is the banquet of the Borgia! Next, the Brothers of Mercy will enter and sing our dirges! At least do me the favor of eating the oysters before it is too late.

Old. (*Who has seized the sheet.*) Plainly, this news is nothing but an uncertain

rumor. Henning will tell us that there is
nothing in it! Sit down with us, and don't
be looking for ghosts!

Bolz. (*Sitting down.*) I sit down, not
because I believe your words, but because
I will not leave the breakfast in the lurch.
Produce Henning! He shall answer for
it.

Old. You hear that he isn't at home.

Bolz. (*Eating eagerly.*) Oh, that will
be a terrible awakening, little Orsini! Bellmaus, pour me a glass! If the story is not
true, however, if this *Coriolanus* has lied,
by the purple in this glass be it sworn!
I will be his murderer! The direst revenge
which an insulted journalist ever took shall
fall upon his head; he shall bleed from
needle thrusts; every pug dog on the street
shall look at him contemptuously and say:
"Fie, Coriolanus, I'll take no bits from
you; no, not even if they were sausage!"
(*Some one knocks. Bolz lays down his
knife.*) Memento mori! It is our grave
diggers! Now for the last oysters and then
farewell, beautiful world! (*Enter Lawyer
Schwarz, Senden, from the door at left.
Door remains open.*)

Schwarz. Humble servant, gentlemen.

Send. Pardon if we disturb you.

Bolz. (*Sitting by the table.*) Not in the
least. This is our usual breakfast, provided

for by contract for a year—fifty oysters and two bottles daily for each member of the staff. Whoever buys the paper has to furnish it.

Schwarz. What brings us here, Professor, is an announcement that Herr Henning should have made to you first. He has preferred to charge me with it.

Old. I await your announcement.

Schwarz. Herr Henning, by a sale, has transferred to me, from yesterday on, all the rights belonging to him as owner of the paper *Union.*

Old. To you, Justizrat?

Schwarz. I confess that I have bought it only as the authorized agent of a third party. Here is the deed of conveyance. There is no secret in it. (*Extends a paper.*)

Old. (*Looking it through, to Bolz.*) It is a contract, attested by a notary in due form—sold for thirty thousand thalers. (*Excitement among the members of the staff.*) Permit me to go to the heart of the matter. Is a change in the political views of the paper obligatory with this change of owners?

Send. (*Coming forward.*) To be sure, Professor. That was the meaning of the sale.

Old. Do I, perhaps, see in you the new proprietor?

Send. Not that, but I have the honor of being on intimate terms with him. You yourself, as well as these gentlemen, have the right to ask that your contracts be fulfilled. Your contracts, as I understand them, call for a six months' notice. It goes without saying that you will continue to draw your salaries till the expiration of that time.

Bolz. (*Rising.*) You are very kind, Herr von Senden. Our contracts give us the right to edit this paper entirely according to our judgment, and likewise to determine, independently, its political policy. We shall, therefore, till the expiration of the next six months, not only continue to draw our salaries, but also to carry on the paper itself for the betterment of the party to which you do not have the honor of belonging.

Send. (*Angrily.*) We shall find means of meeting that!

Old. Calm yourselves! Such conduct would be scarcely fitting! I announce that, under such circumstances, I resign the editorship to-day and release you from all obligations to me.

Bolz. For my part, so be it! I announce the same.

Bell. ⎫
Kämpe. ⎬ We also.
Körner. ⎭

Send. (*To Schwarz.*) You are witness
that the gentlemen voluntarily waive their
rights.

Bolz. (*To the staff.*) Stop, gentlemen!
Do not be too magnanimous. It is right
that you should not interest yourselves further in the paper when your friends withdraw; but why do you wish to relinquish
your pecuniary claims on the new owners?

Bell. I prefer to accept nothing from
them. I will act as you do.

Bolz. (*Patting him on the back.*) Good
idea, my son! We will fight our way
through the world together. What do you
say to a hand-organ, Bellmaus? We will
make all the fairs with it and sing your
songs—I'll turn the crank and you sing.

Old. Since none of you has become
owner of the paper, you will find the question natural at the close of this transac-
tion, to whom have we assigned our rights?

Send. The present owner of the paper
is——

(*Enter Colonel from side door, left.*)

Old. (*Stepping back, frightened.*) Colonel?

Bolz. Oh, now the matter becomes highly tragical!

Col. (*Stepping up to Oldendorf.*) First of all, Professor, be assured that I am not concerned in any of this affair, and I come hither only at the request of the purchaser. Here, just now, I learned what is on hand. I hope you will believe me in this.

Bolz. I, however, find this game out of place, and I insist on knowing who the new proprietor is, who hides himself behind various persons.

(*Enter Adelheid.*)

Adel. (*Entering from side door, left.*) He stands before you!

Bolz. I am going to faint!

Bell. That is a fine joke!

Adel. (*Bowing.*) I greet you gentlemen! (*To the staff.*) Am I right in assuming that these gentlemen have been engaged in the management till now?

Bell. (*Eagerly.*) Yes, indeed, gracious lady! Herr Kämpe for the editorials, Herr Körner for the French and English correspondence, and I for theatre, music, plastic art and that sort of thing.

Adel. I shall be very glad if your principles will permit you to further devote your talents to my newspaper. (*The members of the staff bow.*)

Bell. (*Laying his hand on his heart.*) Gracious lady, to the end of the world under your management!

Adel. (*Smiling and courteously.*) Oh, no—only into this room. (*Points to door at right.*) I need a half hour to collect myself for my new sphere of action.

Bell. (*Leaving.*) That will be a splendid story.

(*Exeunt Bellmaus, Kämpe, Körner.*)

Adel. Professor, you have resigned the management of the paper with a willingness that delights me. (*Meaningly.*) I wish to manage the "Union" in my own way! (*Grasps his hand and leads him to the Colonel.*) Colonel, he is no longer an editor. We have outwitted him. You have your revenge.

Col. (*Opening his arms.*) Come, Oldendorf! What has happened has grieved me since the hour of our separation!

Old. My honored friend!

Adel. (*Pointing to the door, left.*) In there is some one who wishes to share in the reconciliation. Perhaps it is Herr Gabriel Henning.

(*Enter Ida.*)

Ida. (*At side door.*) Eduard! (*Oldendorf hastens to the door, Ida meets him, he embraces her. Both exeunt left, Colonel follows.*)

Adel. (*Politely.*) Before I ask you, Herr von Senden, to become interested in the management of the paper, I beg you to read this correspondence, which I have received as a contribution for my sheet.

Send. (*Throws a glance at it.*) My young lady, I do not know whose indiscretion——

Adel. Do not fear any on my part. I am the proprietress of the paper and (*pointedly*) *I* shall preserve the editorial secrets.

Send. (*Bows.*)

Adel. My I ask you for the document, Justizrat? And will the gentlemen have the goodness to reassure the sellers regarding the result of the business?

(*Bows. Exeunt Senden and Schwarz.*)

Adel. (*After a slight pause.*) Now, Herr Bolz, what shall I do with you?

Bolz. I am prepared for anything. I shall marvel at nothing now. If, next, some one expends a capital of a hundred millions for the purpose of painting all negroes white, or of making Africa four-cornered, I shall not be astonished. If I wake up to-morrow an owl, with two tufts of feathers instead of ears and with a mouse in my beak, I will be content and consider that worse things have already occurred.

Adel. What is the matter with you, Konrad? Are you dissatisfied with me?

Bolz. With you? You have been gen-

erous, as always; only too generous! And
everything would be splendid if only this
whole scene had been impossible. This Senden!

Adel. He will not return. Konrad, I
hold to the party!

Bolz. Triumph! I hear innumerable
angels blowing their trumpets! I stay with
the *Union.*

Adel. Then I have nothing more to decide; but I must make another confession
to you. Even I am not the real owner of
the paper.

Bolz. You are not? Now, by all the
gods, I am at my wits' end. This proprietor is gradually becoming a matter of indif-
ference to me. Whether he is a man, a
will-o'-the-wisp, or the devil Beelzebub
himself, I defy him!

Adel. He is a sort of will-o'-the-wisp, he
is just a little of a devil, and from head to
foot he is a great rascal; for, Konrad, my
friend, lover of my youth, it is you yourself! (*Gives him the document.*)

Bolz. (*Staring for awhile, then reading.*) "Transferred to Konrad Bolz."
"Correct!" "It would be a sort of a
gift." "Cannot be accepted." "Is far
too little." (*Throws the paper aside.*) Get
thee hence, deliberation! (*Falls on his
knees before Adelheid.*) Here I kneel,

Adelheid! What I am saying I know not
for very rapture, for the whole room is
dancing around me. If you would marry
me you would do me the greatest favor in
the world! If you do not wish to, then
give me a slap on the cheek and drive me
away.

Adel. (*Leaning over him.*) I want you.
(*Kissing him.*) It was this cheek——

Bolz. (*Springing up.*) And it is this
mouth! (*Kisses her. They hold each other
close. A short pause.*)

(*Enter the Colonel, Ida, Oldendorf.*)

Col. (*At the door, astonished.*) What
is this?

Bolz. Colonel, it takes place on the re-
sponsibility of the management.

Col. Adelheid, what do I see?

Adel. (*Extending her hand to the Colonel.*) My friend! The promised bride of
a journalist!

(*While Ida and Oldendorf are hastening
from each side towards the pair the curtain
falls.*)

www.ingramcontent.com/pod-product-compliance
Lightning Source LLC
LaVergne TN
LVHW041210080426
835508LV00008B/889